SELAH

Stop. Pause. Listen

SELAH

Stop. Pause. Listen

WENDY MILLER BARTSCH

Facebook: WendyMillerBartschAuthor
Email: wjmillerdesign@yahoo.com

XULON PRESS

Xulon Press
2301 Lucien Way #415
Maitland, FL 32751
407.339.4217
www.xulonpress.com

Paperback ISBN-13: 978-1-66285-604-4
Ebook ISBN-13: 978-1-66285-605-1

Dedication

To my wonderful husband, Brian.

You have always encouraged me to follow my dreams. Without you this book would never have happened. Thank you for all the sacrifices you make to support my ever changing creative talents. Thank you for reading each devotional and giving your honest thoughts. Thank you for being the rock at the end of my kite.

Table of Contents

Introduction

When I was in 7th grade, the teacher showed our class a slide presentation — yes, this was before the days of YouTube and cell phones — of a sunrise by the ocean in Hawaii that he'd taken while on vacation. Most of the class was bored, but I wasn't. I was mesmerized by the beauty of what I saw. It was a God moment for me. It was as if God slowed down time while speaking directly to my heart through those slides.

We were then asked to write a poem interpreting what we just saw. The words poured out like water rushing over a fall. I am told that my poem hung on the bulletin board of the principal's office for many years. I don't remember what I wrote anymore and sadly never got a copy of it. I do remember the awe of that moment and how it took my breath away.

In scripture there is a word with a similar feeling: Selah. It is found 71 times in the Psalms. Scholars don't know exactly what it means. Most believe that it is a musical term indicating to pause, listen, reflect, or to just let the music play while the heart listens.

Too often we find this word an inconvenience or an interruption to reading the psalm. In the past I would often skip over this word thinking it is just an "extra" and not too important. If we admit it, we all have a tendency to jump over it and ignore it. Some translations of the Bible will even omit this word from the psalm to make the reading easier.

I started to dig a little deeper into this word and what I discovered has impacted my time with God. This word begs you to pause and think when the psalmist cries for justice or when he makes observations about the unjust and ungodly. Sometimes it will cause you to recognize your position before God. Ultimately it will turn your heart to worship of the Most High God.

As I read the verses with Selah, I now take a moment to dwell on them. I am learning to take the psalmist's cue and stop, pause, and listen to what the Spirit is saying.

> "This is the person who seeks him,
> who searches for the face of the God
> of Jacob. *Selah*" (Psalm 24:6 GW)

Psalm 3

I dream a lot. Often those dreams are nothing more than the pizza dreams that we all have. They're as varied as my imagination, make little sense, and are a curiosity to me. If I could ever remember them past the few moments of waking, I know I could be a best-selling fiction writer.

A few times in my life I've had dreams where God is speaking. In those dreams there's a lot of allegory for sure. These dreams I remember. These dreams I hang on to, waiting for God to fulfil them. One dream in particular became the proof of God's love a few years later.

The dream was troubling to say the least. It didn't make any sense at the time. In it I was wandering, needing directions, feeling incredibly lost and hopeless. I found a gas station, asked for directions, and was told to take a certain highway. As I wandered down this highway, a storm started, and floodwaters began to cover me to the point that I had to push off the bottom to keep from drowning. I awoke, knowing that God was speaking. Little did I know that in a few years, I would be living this dream. My life fell apart. All I believed in and held dear was torn away from me. I truly was lost and felt hopeless.

But God had a plan. As the pieces of my life came together in new ways, I saw that troubling dream as a blessing from God. I knew that He knew what was coming down the road. Though troubling at the time, it became a source of trust and hope about my future. I could rest, knowing that He was in control.

Psalm 3 contains the first three Selahs in Psalms. As I read the verses surrounding this word, the psalm tells a beautiful story and leaves a wonderful life lesson. It's a progression from complaint to rest to praise and finally a prayer of blessing.

> "O LORD, look how my enemies have increased! Many are attacking me. Many are saying about me, "Even with God on his side, he won't be victorious. *Selah*" (Psalm 3:1-2 GW)

Selah. Stop. Pause. Listen.

With the first Selah David complains to God. His focus is on his problems. Too many enemies, too many attacks, and too many people saying God is against him. This was penned by David when he fled

Jerusalem following his son's attempted takeover of his throne. He was feeling overwhelmingly attacked by family, particularly his son, Absalom. As David cried out, he paused. He took a moment to view things from God's perspective.

Have you ever felt this overwhelmed? I have, many times. But pause. Look at the situation. Not everyone is against you; most of all God is not against you. Take a good look at the problem, a good honest look. Recognize your part in it. Be truthful.

> "But you, O LORD, are a shield that sur-
> rounds me. You are my glory. You hold
> my head high. I call aloud to the LORD,
> and he answers me from his holy
> mountain. *Selah*" (Psalm 3:3-4 GW)

Selah. Stop. Pause. Listen

With the second Selah David remembers that God cares and protects. He starts with "But, you Lord." He remembers who God is to him. He calls God his shield and glory. He knows that as he calls on God, God will hear and will answer.

Do you know, without doubt, that God intimately cares for you? Do you know how precious you are to Him? He knows the day you were conceived. He knows the number of hairs on your head. He thinks you're more precious than the sparrows and the flowers of the field. Rest in this. Let the Holy Spirit's peace flood you like an ocean. Focus on God and what he has done for you. "But you Lord..."

> "Victory belongs to the LORD! May your blessing rest on your people. *Selah*"
> (Psalm 3:8 GW)

Selah. Stop. Pause. Listen.

With the third and final Selah David is at peace. He says that he can rest or sleep peacefully. He knows that God will deliver him. He always does. He always will. David is a warrior and he just can't help but want to say, "sick 'em, Lord!" But he quickly remembers that God will take care of this problem. Miracle of miracles; David totally forgives and prays a blessing on all those involved. "May your blessing be on your people." (Psalm 3:8b GW)

No longer enemies, all is in perspective. God is in control and there is no need for fear or anger or revenge.

When you allow God to be in complete control, you will have complete peace. Rest with the Peace that passes all understanding. Oh, I know that you still want God to vindicate and slay them all. But that is not your decision. Completely forgive. Let it go, and let God handle it. You may not see vindication or justification, but you will have peace! Forgive the situation to the level that you know and want God to forgive you, which should be completely. Then, pray a blessing on the one who is no longer an enemy but a person who God cares about, deeply.

"But you Lord...."

> "Victory belongs to the LORD! May your blessing rest on your people." (Psalm 3:8 GW)

Psalm 4

I remember the day I chewed out a very young and innocent employee at a hardware store. He'd done nothing wrong; he was just a target of my frustration. I ranted on him for a good 15 minutes about how terrible it was that this store would not sell us the floor model that we had driven an hour to come get after I had confirmed over the phone that they had one to sell. I behaved as if it was his entire fault and walked out of that store with my nose in the air without the floor model. Oh, my misguided self-righteousness. This certainly wasn't a proud moment and one that I regret. I still cringe when I remember this incident. I wouldn't have wanted anyone to know I was a Christ follower at that moment. It was clearly not God honoring. It was downright embarrassing.

In Psalm 4 David prays, begging God to answer his prayer. The answer is surprising, and I don't think it's what he expected. But David honestly records God's answer. "You important people, how long are you going to insult my honor? How long are you going to love what is empty and seek what is a lie? *Selah*" (Psalm 4:2 GW) The New Living Translation is even more incriminating as it says, "How long will you people ruin my reputation?"

Selah. Stop. Pause. Listen.

I am deeply struck by this verse. My heart is truly broken. How much of what we do in the name of Christ really isn't honoring Christ at all? Are we so wrapped up in our programs, buildings, and outreaches that we have forgotten God? Is the job that we do or the places we go pulling us away from God? Would we really want God to know what we're doing or saying or watching? Would we want others to know that we're a Christ follower in that moment? This is what Jesus says, "Many will say to me on that day, 'Lord, Lord, didn't we prophesy in your name? Didn't we force out demons and do many miracles by the power and authority of your name?' Then I will tell them publicly, 'I've never known you. Get away from me, you evil people.'" (Matthew 7:22-23 GW)

Ah, but there is a second Selah. "Tremble and do not sin. Think about this on your bed and remain quiet. *Selah*" (Verse 4 GW)

Selah. Stop. Pause. Listen.

This passage literally means to get angry at the dishonoring of God, past and present, and then stop sinning. Change!

As you go to bed, ask the Holy Spirit to examine your heart and actions of the day. Be quiet, and honestly listen for His response. Write it down. David even once prayed for God to forgive the sins that he was not aware of at the moment. Be humble before God about what you're doing, ask forgiveness, and then like the woman caught in adultery, stop doing what dishonors God. You are forgiven.

Read how David finishes this psalm. See the joy and the peace he now has because he has changed his heart and set his focus on God.

> "...Let the light of your presence shine on us, O LORD. You put more joy in my heart than when their grain and new wine increase. I fall asleep in peace the moment I lie down because you alone, O LORD, enable me to live securely." (Psalm 4:6-8 GW)

Psalm 7

I'd never met the woman sitting across the room from me but I could feel her anger towards me. Was I imagining it? I didn't think so. Later that morning I learned she was one of the people I would be working with for the next few months.

A few days later a co-worker came to me privately to talk about the tension she was sensing between me and this woman. I couldn't deny it and was admittedly at a loss as to how to correct it. The tension was draining me too.

Frustrated and hurt, I went for a long walk that afternoon. I cried out to God. I was angry that once again, I was going to have to apologize for something that was not my fault. God why? I was ready to march into that office and just quit then and there. I was steaming with righteous indignation. I was miserable. God had another plan. Through the night, He dealt with the hurt from the past. I awoke that morning feeling like Jacob when he wrestled with the angel all night at the river before reuniting with his brother. I had peace and direction. I knew that God would provide as I took His approach.

In the morning God provided a quiet opportunity for me to talk with her. I would apologize for offending her and causing her a great deal of anxiety and then leave. With that apology she opened up and told me her side of the story. No one had informed her that I was coming until the day before I arrived and she just wasn't prepared for a summer helper. In the end, though we didn't become friends, we did come to a workable truce. I finished my summer and left on good terms. It was a lesson well learned.

Psalm 7 has only one Selah in it at the end of verse 5. But, oh, how powerful it is! "Then let the enemy chase me and catch me. Let him trample my life into the ground. Let him lay my honor in the dust. *Selah*" (Psalm 7:5 GW)

Selah. Stop. Pause. Listen.

What starts out as complaint ends with amazing praise. I love it! You see in this psalm David's thought process as he works through a difficult interpersonal relationship. It's all about Cush. Or is it?

We don't really know who Cush was. Some scholars believe this man was from the tribe of Benjamin, as was Saul. This guy hated David simply because he wasn't a Benjamite. Sound familiar?

At this point, David is in fear for his life. I like that David has an intimate relationship with God. He shows us this relationship by what he says in verses 1-4. He was secure enough to tell God exactly how he was feeling. In this case, he felt attacked. He knew that he himself wasn't perfect. But he also knew that he hadn't done to Cush what was being done to him. David is asking for justice. *Selah*. Pause.

You have an attacker. Maybe it's a coworker whom you feel is trying to undermine you with the boss and others. Maybe it's a family member or friend who just doesn't quite understand what you are doing and why. You feel that you can't say or do anything to make the situation better. In fact, to say or do anything will make it worse. Tell God. He knows. Be honest. Cry out the injustice, the unfairness, and the misunderstandings. Own your part too and ask for God's input. Then, *Selah*. Listen. Write down what you hear the Holy Spirit speaking to your heart.

After his pause David had a better perspective on the situation. David declares God to be a righteous and good Judge, so much so that he asks God to judge his motives as well. In verse 11 David declares, "God is a fair judge."

"What can we say about all of this? If God is for us, who can be against us? The one who loves us gives us an overwhelming victory in all these difficulties. I am convinced that nothing can ever separate us from God's love which Christ Jesus our Lord shows us. We can't be separated by death or life, by angels or rulers, by anything in the present or anything in the future, by forces or powers in the world above or in the world below, or by anything else in creation." (Romans 8:31, 37-39 GW)

When all is said and done, when David has spent time with God he closes with praise. Today, close your time with David's words of praise...

> "I will give thanks to the LORD for his righteousness. I will make music to praise the name of the LORD Most High." (Psalm 7:17 GW)

Psalm 24, Part One

It starts with a game of Peek-a-Boo. With hands over my face, I hide from my infant child. As I take my hands away, my infant's face lights up and peals of giggles break forth. As she gets older, we play Hide-and-Seek. Again, the joy of searching and the joy of being found register across her face and mine. It is a simple game, but it is also so much more. It creates an inseparable bond that continues for the rest of our lives. She knows that I am always there for her. We look forward to our times together, to touching, to hearing each other's voices. There is an intimacy in this parent/child bond that is like no other.

> "This is the person who seeks him,
> who searches for the face of the God
> of Jacob. *Selah*" (Psalm 24:6 GW)

Selah. Stop. Pause. Listen.

I don't want to just know God, that is to have head knowledge about God. This would be like studying about a person in history. You can know where they lived, who their parents were, what they did, and why they are famous or infamous. But you haven't sat down and had a face-to-face conversation with them. You haven't spent time with them personally. You can't know them intimately.

> "Who may go up the LORD's mountain? Who may stand in his holy place? The one who has clean hands and a pure heart and does not long for what is false nor lie when he is under oath. This person will receive a blessing from the LORD and righteousness from God, his savior. This is the person who seeks him, who searches for the face of the God of Jacob. *Selah*" (Psalm 24:3-6 GW)

Selah. Stop. Pause. Listen.

I want to know God intimately, personally. I want to sit face-to-face with Him as the Psalm says. I want to be in His presence. I want to go before God in prayer. But not just with prayer, with worship also. Worship is that place of honoring God for who He is. It's desiring to spend time with Him like Mary who chose to sit at the Lord's feet in Luke 10:39. Worship is changing my life for Him.

> "O God, you are my God; I earnestly search for you. My soul thirsts for you; my whole body longs for you in this parched and weary land where there is no water. I have seen you in your sanctuary and gazed upon your power and glory. Your unfailing love is better than life itself; how I praise you!" (Psalm 63:1–3 NLT).

The best part of all this is that as I seek (search, desire) for God's intimate presence, He responds in kind. He removes His hands from his face, like the game of Peek-a-Boo, and we look at each other, closely. We bond, an inseparable, intimate bond. We know each other.

> "I love those who love me, and those who seek me find me" (Proverbs 8:17 NIV). "You will seek me and find me when you seek me with all your heart" (Jeremiah 29:13 NIV).

Psalm 24, Part Two

Ever have one of those light bulb moments? You know, the "ah-ha". That moment when it all comes clear, when everything falls into place, and you finally understand. I had one of those moments this spring while driving over the mountain pass. I could see for miles up there. The song "Awesome God" came on the radio and all of a sudden, I just couldn't contain the joy. I started to shout and praise God while still managing to stay buckled in and focused on the road. I was in God's awesome presence. I could understand His awesomeness, His love, His indescribable creation power.

David was searching for the face of God. He wanted God's presence, completely. He wanted to know God intimately. No head knowledge for him. Deeper, more real, more passionate, that's what he was after. Then it happened. Wow! True recognition! This final Selah of psalm 24 was David's "ah-ha" moment. Feel his excitement, his uncontainable joy as he realizes totally who God is. Watch his worship explode.

> "Who, then, is this king of glory? The
> LORD of Armies is the king of glory!
> *Selah*" (Psalm 24:10 GW)

Selah. Stop. Pause. Listen.

One short statement, but oh, so powerful. Our English language cannot express the depth of intimate knowledge and worship that is contained here. Let me elaborate.

He is a glorious God, a God of abundance, riches, splendor, and honor! He is King of Glory! He is the Lord of Armies! He is the Lord of Hosts of Angels! He is the Lord of all Creation! He can do anything! He is! "Who, then, is this king of glory? The LORD of Armies is the king of glory! *Selah*" (Psalm 24:10 GW)

Jesus asked his famous question of his disciples, "Who do you say that I am?" At first, they spouted off the head knowledge of what the prevailing opinions were. Jesus asked again, "Who do you say I am? Peter nailed it. "You are the Messiah, the Son of the living God!" (Matthew 16:16 GW) One short statement that contains all there is to know about Jesus and God. Intimate, passionate worship.

"You alone are the LORD. You made the heavens, even the highest heavens, and all their starry host, the earth and all that is on it, the seas and all that is in them. You give life to everything, and the multitudes of heaven worship you." (Nehemiah 9:6 NIV)

Awesome!

Psalm 39

I magine with me for a moment. You have a very big empty bucket in front of you. Now, take an eyedropper and put one drop of water in this bucket. That drop is hardly noticeable, right? In fact, it disappears as it spreads out and quickly dries on the bottom of this bucket. That is your life in comparison to eternity. As David says, "Indeed, you have made the length of my days only a few inches. My life span is nothing compared to yours. Certainly, everyone alive is like a whisper in the wind. *Selah*" (Psalm 39:5 GW)

Selah. Stop. Pause. Listen.

David is wrestling with a very big problem in Psalm 39. We don't know exactly what it was or when this took place in his life. We can only experience his heart process with God.

From verse 10 we learn that David is sick. I like that he understood that this was God's way of getting his attention and he doesn't blame God for it

(Verse 11). Sometimes we are so determined to do things our own way that we ignore God. Then, one day, we are flat on our backs, jobless, directionless, with nothing but time to think and contemplate. Our plans did not work out as we expected. God now has our full attention.

Our first reaction is often to yell at God and tell everyone within earshot about the injustice that has come upon us because this shouldn't have happened. We tell ourselves that we are good Christians and don't deserve this. But David chose the higher, more difficult ground. David didn't talk about his sickness with anyone. He kept to himself. He needed time to process what was taking place in his life. He did not want to give anyone a reason to get angry at God. (verses 1-3)

When he finally did talk in verse 4, he went straight to God. "Teach me, O LORD, about the end of my life. Teach me about the number of days I have left so that I may know how temporary my life is." (Psalm 39:4 GW) He is getting perspective on this. He is seeking answers. And he finds it in verse 5, "Indeed, you have made the length of my days only a few inches. My life span is nothing compared to yours. Certainly, everyone alive is like a whisper in the wind. *Selah*" (Psalm 39:5 GW)

Selah. Stop. Pause. Listen.

This was his Selah moment. This life is short in comparison to eternity. It is a drop in the bucket. David realized that it was more important to be focused on God and not his problem. He exclaims in verse 7, "And now, Lord, what am I waiting for? My hope is in you!" God will take care of it. He still asks God to heal the sickness, as we should and do. But the focus was no longer on the problem. It was now on God.

> "Stop storing up treasures for your-selves on earth, where moths and rust destroy and thieves break in and steal. Instead, store up treasures for your-selves in heaven, where moths and rust don't destroy and thieves don't break in and steal. Your heart will be where your treasure is." (Matthew 6:19-21 GW)

Psalm 44

I loved milking my cow. She was my pet. We had a bond. The steady rhythmic flow and sound of the milk going into the pail was relaxing and soothing. I could think here, uninterrupted. That barn was my sanctuary. It was my hiding place, my quiet place. It was the place I talked with God. One day, I cried out in desperation, "Don't let go of me. If you let go, I have nothing." I was struggling. Life was not pleasant for me then. I couldn't hang on to God myself any longer. God faithfully answered that desperate prayer that day and has never let go of me.

Psalm 44 is an interesting prayer. It was written by one of Korah's descendants. It reminds me of that desperate prayer that day.

He starts out by remembering how God gave them their Promised Land. Verse 3 says it so well. "It was not with their swords that they took possession of the land. They did not gain victory with their own strength. It was your right hand, your arm, and the light of your presence that did it, because you were pleased with them." (Psalm 44:3 GW) It was God, all God.

In verses 4-8, He goes on to praise God. He recognizes that it is not by his strength or abilities that God rescues. It is only God. And then, "All day long we praise our God. We give thanks to you forever. *Selah*" (Psalm 44:8 GW)

Selah. Stop. Pause. Listen.

There it is. Praise. Forever praise. With this Selah, this pause, we remember that God is present. God is there, always, no matter what happens, no matter where we are God is there.

Now he gets down to business. The remainder of the psalm is his cry for understanding. Things are not going well. He is confused that if Israel has not forgotten God, why has God seemingly forgotten them? In all this, he is not angry with God. Instead, he finishes with, "Arise! Help us! Rescue us because of your mercy!" (Verse 26 GW) His prayer is short, to the point, and without elaboration. His trust is secure. He relies on God's mercy, kindness, compassion, and faithfulness.

Remember all that God has done for you. Remember the times when God rescued you, provided for you, and saved you. Remember that you cannot do anything in your own strength, only with

God's strength. And when you feel that you can hang on no longer, cry out, "Arise! Help me! Rescue me because of your mercy!"

> "But I walk with integrity. Rescue me, and have pity on me. My feet stand on level ground. I will praise the LORD with the choirs in worship." (Psalm 26:11-12 GW)

Psalm 46

I am told that I am a bit of a control freak. Honestly, I don't see it. I just like to know how things are going to turn out. I like to plan my day. I like telling my husband Brian what to do. I am also spontaneous, but usually on my terms. I get a bit pouty when things don't go as I have planned. Okay, I'm a control freak.

For us controllers, God has a better plan. He says, "I rule the nations. I rule the earth." (Psalm 46:10b GW) You mean, I can't make my little spot on the world conform to my plans? Nope. That's God's department. Let's look at Psalm 46. It is another Selah moment.

> "God is our refuge and strength, an ever-present help in times of trouble. That is why we are not afraid even when the earth quakes or the mountains topple into the depths of the sea. Water roars and foams, and mountains

shake at the surging waves. *Selah*"
(Psalm 46:1-3)

Selah. Stop Pause. Listen.

Control issues are often rooted in fear. We are afraid to fail. We don't like not knowing how the end will turn out. We want to be secure. This is when we need to remember who is in control. The world around us will be in turmoil, that is a given. But as verses 1-3 says, God is there, always, no matter what happens. You do not need to be afraid.

Verses 4-6 show us that God is on His throne, always. He is in control. This is where the next Selah comes in. It is so impacting that it is repeated as the last verse too. "The LORD of Armies is with us. The God of Jacob is our stronghold. *Selah*" (Psalm 46:7&11 GW)

Selah. Stop. Pause. Listen.

This God of ours, who created us and the whole world, who commands an army of angels, is with us! God is in the house, Amen! You cannot stop the bad stuff happening. You cannot add a single moment to your life. God has your life in his hands. "Let go of your concerns! Then you will know that I am God. I rule the nations. I rule the earth." (Psalm 46:10 GW)

"Turn all your anxiety over to God because he cares for you. Keep your mind clear, and be alert. Your opponent the devil is prowling around like a roaring lion as he looks for someone to devour. Be firm in the faith and resist him, knowing that other believers throughout the world are going through the same kind of suffering. God, who shows you his kindness and who has called you through Christ Jesus to his eternal glory, will restore you, strengthen you, make you strong, and support you as you suffer for a little while. Power belongs to him forever. Amen." (1Peter 5:7-11 GW)

Psalm 47

The movie "Uptown Girls" is the story of Molly, a guileless young woman who hasn't quite grown up, living off her inheritance from her deceased father. Until, one morning she is penniless and homeless because the accountant took it all. She is rudely thrust into reality and has to find her way in the world.

If you could choose an inheritance for your children, what would you choose? Would it be money, land, a good moral character? Most of us would say the last one, and maybe money. God also has chosen an inheritance for us.

> "He chooses our inheritance for us, the
> pride of Jacob, whom he loved. *Selah*"
> (Psalm 47:4 GW)

Selah. Stop. Pause. Listen.

This psalm joyfully sings about God's authority over the earth, over man, and over nations and rulers.

The joy is contagious. You can just feel the joy as it was being written. Then in verse 4, take a close look at the joyful promises of this verse.

The first promise, "His choice." "Even before he made the world, God loved us and chose us in Christ to be holy and without fault in his eyes." (Ephesians 1:4 NLT) "God also decided ahead of time to choose us through Christ according to his plan, which makes everything work the way he intends. He planned all of this so that we who had already focused our hope on Christ would praise him and give him glory." (Ephesians 1:11-12 GW)

The second promise, "Our inheritance." "We have been born into a new life which has an inheritance that can't be destroyed or corrupted and can't fade away. That inheritance is kept in heaven for you, since you are guarded by God's power through faith for a salvation that is ready to be revealed at the end of time." (1 Peter 1:4-5 GW) "And everyone who gave up homes, brothers or sisters, father, mother, children, or fields because of my name will receive a hundred times more and will inherit eternal life." (Matthew 19:29 GW)

The third promise, "His love." "I am convinced that nothing can ever separate us from God's love which Christ Jesus our Lord shows us. We can't be separated by death or life, by angels or rulers, by anything in the present or anything in the future, by forces or powers in the world above or in the world below, or by anything else in creation." (Romans 8:38-39 GW)

He chooses you. Out of all the people in the world, God chose you. God wanted you with all your imperfections and faults.

He has an inheritance for you. You have a place, a possession in heaven just for you. In this life you have already inherited a new life and the chance to have a relationship with Christ.

And why all this? Because He loves you. Enough said. You can't earn it. You just have to accept it. He loves you!

> "I pray that the glorious Father, the God of our Lord Jesus Christ, would give you a spirit of wisdom and revelation as you come to know Christ better. Then you will have deeper insight. You will know the confidence that he calls you to have and the glorious wealth that God's people will inherit." (Ephesians 1:17-18 GW)

Psalm 49

I am a spender. I can usually think of a hundred ways to spend a dollar. That extra change in my wallet? Gone, spent. Why break a five? When you are also married to a spender, things can get interesting.

My sister and brother on the other hand are savers. Growing up, my brother had a bowl on his dresser that was always filled with quarters. My sister had a bank for each coin, and they actually had coins in them! I once asked her to hang on to some of my money and not give it to me no matter what. By the end of the week, I wanted it, and of course she wouldn't give it back. It got heated. Mom intervened and I got my money. I should have let her continue to hang onto it for me.

For those of you who put your trust in how much you have in the bank, this one is for you. Psalm 49 is a wonderful salvation message just for you.

"But mortals will not continue here
with what they treasure. They are like

animals that die. This is the final outcome for fools and their followers who
are delighted by what they say: *Selah*."
(Psalm 49:12-13 GW)

Selah. Stop. Pause. Listen.

The psalmist has seen what happens when all
a person's trust is in their wealth. He has seen the
abuses of wealth. "They trust their riches and brag
about their abundant wealth." (Psalm 49:6) "You
have hoarded wealth in the last days. You have lived
on earth in luxury and self-indulgence. You have fattened yourselves in the day of slaughter." (James
5:3 & 5 NIV)

The psalm goes on to say that no amount of
money can get you out of hell. No amount of good
deeds will earn you a place in heaven. "No one can
ever buy back another person or pay God a ransom
for his life. The price to be paid for his soul is too
costly. Even though he blesses himself while he
is alive (and they praise you when you do well for
yourself), he must join the generation of his ances-
tors, who will never see light again" (Psalm 49:7-8,
18-19 GW) "Jesus answered, "If you want to be perfect, go, sell your possessions, and give to the poor,
and you will have treasure in heaven. Then come,
follow me." When the young man heard this, he went

away sad, because he had great wealth." (Matthew 19:21-22 NIV)

There is hope. "But God will buy me back from the power of hell because he will take me. *Selah*" (Psalm 49:15 GW)

Selah. Stop Pause. Listen.

This is the reason Jesus came. Money will not get you into heaven. Good deeds will not get you into heaven. Sacrifices will not get you into heaven. Only God, only Jesus can buy you. He paid with his life on the cross. "For God so loved the world that he gave his one and only Son, that whoever believes in him shall not perish but have eternal life. Whoever believes in him is not condemned, but whoever does not believe stands condemned already because they have not believed in the name of God's one and only Son." (John 3:16 & 18 NIV)

All the riches in the world will not keep you from death. You cannot cheat it. It will happen. You cannot buy your way into heaven. But you can believe in Jesus, the Son of God, and put your treasure with Him.

> "Do not store up for yourselves trea-
> sures on earth, where moths and
> vermin destroy, and where thieves
> break in and steal. But store up for

yourselves treasures in heaven, where moths and vermin do not destroy, and where thieves do not break in and steal. For where your treasure is, there your heart will be also." (Matthew 6:19-21 NIV)

Psalm 50

"The heavens announce his righteousness because God is the judge. *Selah*"
(Psalm 50:6 GW)

Selah. Stop. Pause. Listen.

Judgement, worship, praise, sacrifice, thanksgiving. Out of these, we struggle the most with
judgement. We have all been on the receiving end
of unjust judgement. We have also participated in
unjust judgements. Each day we make judgements
about what is good or bad, acceptable and unaccept-
able, who is right and who is wrong. We struggle with
this one word, this action, almost daily. We struggle
with understanding God as a just judge when things
don't turn out the way we think it should have.

We have seen unprecedented fires, earthquakes,
hurricanes, extreme heatwaves, droughts, and
other major natural disasters throughout the world
causing major destruction and devastation. Do these

things cause you to turn to God? If so, how, or why do you go to God? Honestly, most of us cry out for God to stop or intervene in these disasters because they are affecting our plans or happiness. Maybe instead of asking for these things to stop, we need to ask for God's heart on why these things are happening. Maybe God wants our attention.

Psalm 50 has caused me to stop and contemplate, to question my motives, my prayers, my "sacrifices." It is a psalm judging the godly and the ungodly. Open your Bible to this wonderful psalm and read with me. Let's look at God's judgement of the godly in verses 7-15.

God owns it all. He created this world and everything in it. We cannot give back to God what is already his. He is not upset here with our sacrifice but the manner in which the sacrifices are offered. We are not doing God a favor with our church attendance or financial giving or frugal living. It is about the heart, always the heart. It is about the thanksgiving and the willing obedient trust of doing these things. It is about honoring God. We honor God with our sacrifice of church attendance and our time. We honor God with our financial and physical giving. Live your life to bring honor to God whether that is in a mansion or a rundown shack. Not sure? Ask God if what you are doing is bringing Him honor. Be prepared for the answer; it could change your life.

The next verses, 16-22, are directed at the ungodly and those who follow God according to their own set of rules and opinions. Just because God has not immediately condemned your actions or behavior does not mean you have gotten away with it or that God is condoning it.

Finally, "Whoever offers thanks as a sacrifice honors me. I will let everyone who continues in my way see the salvation that comes from God." (Psalm 50:23 GW) Thanking God in the misery of life is not easy. I think that is why it is a sacrifice. Immediate results or answers are not guaranteed. But a thankful and willing heart will be rewarded. People will see your trust in God and will start to ask questions.

> "So get rid of every kind of evil, every kind of deception, hypocrisy, jealousy, and every kind of slander. Desire God's pure word as newborn babies desire milk. Then you will grow in your salvation. Certainly you have tasted that the Lord is good! So offer spiritual sacrifices that God accepts through Jesus Christ. ... you are chosen people, a royal priesthood, a holy nation, people who belong to God. You were chosen to tell about the excellent qualities of God, who called you out of darkness

into his marvelous light." (2 Peter
2:1-3, 5b, 9 GW)

Psalm 52

D o you ever feel like you live in a world gone mad? You have only to watch the evening news to see the violent, self-centered, and destructive happenings around the world. There are days when I feel like Lot living in the midst of unimaginable depravity and violence. Sadly, the current happenings in the world have even polarized the Christian community.

Psalm 52 gives us two Selahs in which David ponders evil, its end result, and finally the believer's choice. David tells us the inspiration for this psalm is concerning Doeg, the man who betrayed him to Saul and then slew 85 innocent priests and their families. The story can be found in 1 Samuel chapters 21 and 22.

> "You prefer evil to good. You prefer lying to speaking the truth. *Selah*. But God will ruin you forever. He will grab you and drag you out of your tent. He

will pull your roots out of this world of
the living. *Selah*" (Psalm 53:3&5 GW)

Selah. Stop. Pause. Listen.

These are harsh words for sure, yet they are truth.
Doeg was the worst kind of depravity. He bragged,
lied, and threatened and enjoyed doing so. We know
from 1 Samuel that he killed without compulsion.
His end would be complete destruction. Like a dead
tree that is cut down and has its roots dug out, there
would be no second chance and no bargaining done.
This is the person who is so far from God's ways
that there is little hope of ever turning around. "You
must understand this: In the last days there will be
violent periods of time. People will be selfish and
love money. They will brag, be arrogant, and use abusive language. They will curse their parents, show no
gratitude, have no respect for what is holy, and lack
normal affection for their families. They will refuse
to make peace with anyone. They will be slanderous,
lack self-control, be brutal, and have no love for what
is good. They will be traitors. They will be reckless
and conceited. They will love pleasure rather than
God. They will appear to have a godly life, but they
will not let its power change them." (2 Timothy 3:1-5
GW) Sadly there are those who prefer evil, lying and

bragging about doing wrong along with a host of other unseemly behavior. Evil has become good.

What are we to do? David concludes with four truths for the believer. "But I am like a large olive tree in God's house. I trust the mercy of God forever and ever. I will give thanks to you forever for what you have done. In the presence of your godly people, I will wait with hope in your good name." (Psalm 52:8-9 GW)

First, be rooted in God. Trust Him above all else. Know that God is ultimately in control and has a hope and a future for you. You can flourish and grow like a well-watered tree when you stay intimately connected to God.

Second be thankful. Don't let the evil around you destroy your confidence and faith in God. God is good. Thank Him in the midst of all the turmoil and unfairness and destruction.

Third, wait on God. Your strength and peace come from patiently waiting, that is time spent in prayer, meditation, and study. Get to know God intimately and you won't be focused on the evil around you.

Fourth, stay connected to God's people. Choose to hang out with other Christ followers who will strengthen you, encourage you, and challenge you to grow in Christ.

"This is the reason I kneel in the presence of the Father from whom all the family in heaven and on earth receives its name. I'm asking God to give you a gift from the wealth of his glory. I pray that he would give you inner strength and power through his Spirit. Then Christ will live in you through faith. I also pray that love may be the ground into which you sink your roots and on which you have your foundation. This way, with all of God's people, you will be able to understand how wide, long, high, and deep his love is. You will know Christ's love, which goes far beyond any knowledge. I am praying this so that you may be completely filled with God." (Ephesians 3:14-19 GW)

Psalm 54

Who are your heroes? You know the people in your life that you admire, respect, and look to for wisdom and advice. I have been blessed to have had several in my life. My parents, they challenged me to grow and be strong and follow my dreams. My piano teacher, she not only taught me music but led me to Christ and became a spiritual mentor. The teachers who encouraged me to do better academically and pushed me. And the many people whom I have had the honor to call friend because they taught me to laugh, or cried with me, or challenged me to grow as a believer, or stood with me through the dark days.

David had a hero too. His was God. In Psalm 54, he uses three different words to describe God. Each has a different relationship and understanding of who God is. David was again reaching out to God over the difficulties in his life. This time it was betrayal by a number of people in Ziph. My guess is that these were the leaders fearing for the safety of the city. What I like about this psalm is David's use of the different words for God. Let's unpack this.

Verses 1,2,3 and 4 use Elohim in the plural form for the supreme God. Verse 4 also uses Adonai, the proper name for God meaning "my Lord" which is spoken in place of Yahweh in a Jewish display of deep respect. Verse 6 uses Jehovah, the existing one, the proper name of the one true God. It is the Jewish national name of God. David moves through this psalm from an impersonal to a personal relationship with God.

> "O God (*Elohim, the supreme God*), save me by your name and defend me with your might. O God (*Elohim, the supreme God*), hear my prayer, and open your ears to the words from my mouth. Strangers have attacked me. Ruthless people seek my life. They do not think about God (*Elohim, the supreme God*)" *Selah* (Psalm 54:1-3 GW)

Selah. Stop. Pause. Listen.

Got trouble? Get God. How often have you felt attacked, maybe even unjustly attacked over something you had little control over? Cry out to God!

Don't hold back. He is listening. He cares. Tell Him exactly how you are feeling, just as David did here. Then, pause. Let God show you his perspective and his plan. See how your heart changes and peace floods in. Let God be your hero.

"God (*Elohim, the supreme God*) is my helper! The Lord (*Adonai, my Lord*) is the provider for my life. My enemies spy on me. Pay them back with evil. Destroy them with your truth! I will make a sacrifice to you along with a freewill offering. I will give thanks to your good name, O LORD. (*Jehovah, the existing one*) Your name rescues me from every trouble. My eyes will gloat over my enemies." (Psalm 54:4-7 GW)

"My God (*the supreme divinity, the Godhead, trinity, all encompassing*) will richly fill your every need in a glorious way through Christ Jesus. Glory belongs to our God and Father forever! Amen." (Philippians 4:19-20 GW)

(Italics in parenthesis added for emphasis)

Psalm 57

When my life fell apart all those years ago, I made a decision then that would change who I was and the direction my life would take. I chose to not be defined as a victim or a survivor. This wasn't ignoring what I had gone through and pretending it had never happened. It was choosing to live a life that accepted the bad and to honor and glorify God through it and with it. I fought through anger, bitterness, hopelessness, and emptiness. I walked through grief. I found comfort in David's psalms.

What I like about David and his writing of the psalms is his blunt honesty. He tells it like it is. Made a mistake? He admits it. Wants his enemies annihilated? He admits it. Feeling trapped, lost, and hopeless? He searches for God. Knows that God will help him and take care of him? Absolutely he admits it. Does he give God all the glory? Always.

In Psalm 57 you can see David working through another problem. He is now living in a cave, coming to terms with his situation, being hunted by Saul, surrounded by liars and cheats, and seeking God's help. There are two Selahs in this psalm.

> "He sends his help from heaven and saves me. He disgraces the one who is harassing me. *Selah*" (Psalm 57:3 GW) "My enemies spread out a net to catch me. (My soul is bowed down.) They dug a pit to trap me, but then they fell into it. *Selah*" (Psalm 57:6 GW)

Selah. Stop. Pause. Listen.

David knew that his only help would ultimately come from God and he was humbled by this knowledge. I think he inserted these Selahs to just take a moment and really contemplate this. It might have been one of those "ah-ha" moments for him. He came to understand that even though the trials, troubles, and uncomfortable life were all around him, God was still worth glorifying. He wasn't complaining about all the wrong done to him nor was he asking God to take the trial away. Instead he chose to honor God in the midst of it. "You prepare a banquet for me while my enemies watch." (Psalm 23:5 GW)

The fear did not automatically go away. His problems didn't suddenly vanish because he praised God. He was not taken out of the cave and instantly put on the throne. But he wanted the world to know that God is always worthy of praise. "My heart is confident, O God. My heart is confident. I want to sing and make music. Wake up, my soul! Wake up, harp and lyre! I want to wake up at dawn. I want to give thanks to you among the people, O Lord. I want to make music to praise you among the nations because your mercy is as high as the heavens. Your truth reaches the skies." (Psalm 57:7-10 GW) He chose not to be a victim of his circumstances but to be a God worshipper.

I do not want to minimize what you have gone through. Your pain is real and very deep. But I do want to suggest there is a better way. It is okay to grieve and to hurt, but don't let it define you. You are not a victim who worships God. You are a God worshipper, a Jesus follower who was victimized. Satan wanted to take you out. God chose you for his glory.

> "Do not be afraid, because I have reclaimed you. I have called you by name; you are mine. When you go through the sea, I am with you. When you go through rivers, they will not sweep you away. When you walk through fire, you will not be burned, and the flames will not harm you. I am

the L ORD your God, the Holy One of
Israel, your Savior." (Isaiah 43:1-3 GW)

Psalm 59

I t was night. The house was surrounded by men seeking David's life for a reward. Men for hire, money meant everything to them. It didn't matter to them that the man they were hunting was innocent. He could hear their voices just outside, sneering with derisive laughter. They were telling the story told to them and to them that was all that mattered.

There seemed to be no escape. What had he done to deserve such treatment? He could think of no wrong. His work, his loyalty was unquestionable. Many could attest to it. Yet here he was, facing unjust arrest and certain death. Then his wife had an idea; run and live. Surely this could work long enough to prove his innocence. Together his wife and servants lowered him through the window.

Psalm 59 was written about the beginning of David's long journey as a fugitive from King Saul. You can read about it in 1 Samuel 19:11-18. This psalm has two Selahs in it. It would be hard to focus on just two verses without examining each section.

> "O LORD God of Armies, God of
> Israel, arise to punish all the nations.
> Have no pity on any traitors. *Selah*"

(Psalm 59:5 GW)

Selah. Stop. Pause. Listen.

Verses 1- 5 contain the first Selah. Here David
cries out to God for help. Words of "rescue me, protect me, save me, rise up and help me" come from
the heart. These are words not just of an earthly
sense but hold more of a spiritual sense. David cries
for his spirit to be set apart to a safe place in God.
David is not asking for momentary physical help. He
is focusing on God.

> "Destroy them in your rage. Destroy
> them until not one of them is left.
> Then they will know that God rules
> Jacob to the ends of the earth. *Selah*"

(Psalm 59:13 GW)

Selah. Stop. Pause. Listen.

Verses 11-13 contain the second Selah. David
isn't asking God to exact revenge on his enemies.
Instead, his focus is on God and telling through this
psalm how much God hates evil. He is concerned

about how this evil and the punishment will affect all Israel. His desire is not just for punishment but to see a punishment that will ultimately bring God glory and honor by displaying His justice.

Bad things do happen to good people. We all initially get rocked by the suddenness of disaster. Cancer, death, broken relationships, and job loss affect us all. We can learn from David that it is all about focus.

When you go before God with the bad things of life, where is your focus? Are you looking for God to remove the problem? Are you trying to bargain with God? Are you trying to seek God in the problem? If it involves a boss, coworker, friend, or family member are you praying for revenge in the form of some kind of disaster upon the other person? Or are you concerned about them and their relationship with the Father? Are you seeking a godly solution? Is your attitude solely about you and your situation? Are you concerned about how others around you will view it? Is your goal through this to bring glory to God?

When the door is closed and no one is around, pray, scream, cry, and pour out your heart to God. Then let your merciful and kind Father God in heaven guide you. Let this troubling time bring glory to God and new life to you.

"The LORD is a stronghold for the oppressed, a stronghold in times of trouble. Those who know your name trust you, O LORD, because you have never deserted those who seek your help." (Psalm 9:9-10 GW)

"But I will sing about your strength. In the morning I will joyfully sing about your mercy. You have been my stronghold and a place of safety in times of trouble. O my strength, I will make music to praise you! God is my stronghold, my merciful God!" (Psalm 59:16-17 GW)

Psalm 60

When I was a young girl, my town formed a girls softball league. It was named the Powderpuff league. Don't laugh; it was pink t-shirts and all. For my sister who lived to play sports, this was a chance to play ball. For me, well I kept hoping to figure a way out of it. I couldn't hit, I couldn't catch, and I was a guaranteed out for the other team. Each team had a name that was ultra-feminine. I don't remember our team's name. I have blocked it from memory. Our team had a great coach who taught us the importance of good sportsmanship. I think our party at the end of the season wasn't about how well we played but about how we became a team and had fun in the process.

Psalm 60 is a lesson David wrote to teach us about being on God's team and rallying under God's banner. David battled for his kingdom. It wasn't all glory and good times. Joab was being defeated by the Edomites, so David went before God to understand why. And through this we get another Selah moment.

"Yet, you have raised a flag for those who
fear you so that they can rally to it when
attacked by bows and arrows. *Selah*"
(Psalm 60:4 GW)

Selah. Stop. Pause. Listen.

What is the purpose of a flag, or banner? In war,
before our modern technology it was used for sig-
naling directions to the troops and let the soldiers
know where their side was in the battle. It was a rallying point, the place to go to when in need. Think of
team sports and their banners. If you go to a game,
you can identify each team's fans by the colors they
wear and the banners they wave. That banner creates a kind of unity among fans.

Moses, when Israel was fighting the Amalekites,
stood high above the battle with the staff in his hand.
As long as the staff was raised, Israel was winning.
When the battle was over, "Moses built an altar and
called it The LORD Is My Banner." (Exodus 17:15
GW) Moses wanted them to know that God united
and protected them and they won because God was
fighting for them.

David knew the importance of God's banner.
Instead of relying on his own strength or the
strength of his troops, he wanted God's strength.
David understood that when the battle wasn't going

as expected, there was a spiritual problem among the troops. He rallied them to God's flag. He went to God for answers. "Give us help against the enemy because human assistance is worthless. With God we will display great strength. He will trample our enemies." (Psalm 60:11-12 GW) "Some rely on chariots and others on horses, but we will boast in the name of the LORD our God. They will sink to their knees and fall, but we will rise and stand firm." (Psalm 20:7-8 GW) Joab won the battle when their focus was back on God.

For the Christ follower, God is your banner. When you are being attacked, when difficulties bombard you, you can rally under God's banner, his flag, not only for protection but more importantly for direction. Instead of trying to get out of the difficulty, learn to run to God in the midst of it. God may very well have allowed this life battle for a few reasons. First and most importantly it is for His glory and honor. Second, because you have started relying on yourself instead of God. Third, simply to teach you and help you grow as a believer.

> "We will joyfully sing about your victory. We will wave our flags in the name of our God." (Psalm 20:5 GW) "Then everyone gathered here will know that the LORD can save without

sword or spear, because the LORD determines every battle's outcome." (1 Samuel 17:47 GW)

Psalm 61

I was lonely, feeling desperately lost, and not sure of how I would get through the day, the week, or years. All I could do was cry out, "God, please don't let go of me." I could relate to the song Amy Grant sang, "The Warrior is a Child" by <u>Gary Valenciano</u>. In it, she sings of how the warrior is strong and well protected in her armor and seemingly invincible to those around her. Yet, in the moments not in front of the world, when the armor is off, she cries and clings to Jesus because in reality, she feels as helpless as a child in need of protection. I have never forgotten that desperate cry. I was at the end of my rope, but God was tightly clutching my hand. Today, I know that God was hanging on to me then like a father cradling his wounded child. I can be strong in the face of problems because God is always protecting me.

David was a man, strong in faith and battle, valiant, and a slayer of giants. People wanted to hang out with David. Yet, in psalm 61, we see his vulnerability, his feeling of being at the end of his rope. He knew that he needed God who was above him, who was stronger than him, and whom he could cling to. Through his despondency David hung on to the undeniable fact that God was always there for him.

> "I would like to be a guest in your
> tent forever and to take refuge under
> the protection of your wings. *Selah*"
> (Psalm 61:4 GW)

Selah. Stop. Pause. Listen.

David is not asking God to take the problems away. He is acknowledging that God will protect him and be with him through the problems. He knows that God is the only place of rest and hiding from the deluge of the world that demanded so much from him. He understood the importance of the safe place of time spent alone with just God and him, the sheltered place of refuge.

Many times David prayed this prayer. "Hide me in the shadow of your wings." (Psalm 17:8 GW) "I have asked one thing from the LORD. This I will seek: to remain in the LORD's house all the days of my life in order to gaze at the LORD's beauty and to search for an answer in his temple He hides me in his shelter when there is trouble. He keeps me hidden in his tent. He sets me high on a rock." (Psalm 27:4-5 GW)

"You are my hiding place and my shield. My hope is based on your word." (Psalm 119:114 GW)

I love how David finishes this psalm. After he has spent that time in God's presence, he comes out singing. Refreshed and restored, he is ready to face another battle. "You have given me the inheritance that belongs to those who fear your name. I will make music to praise your name forever, as I keep my vows day after day." (Psalm 61:5 & 8 GW)

Being a Christ follower doesn't mean that you will be problem free. What is does mean is that you have a God who is far above you and has a much different perspective on what you are going through. When life's problems start to overwhelm you, when you feel like you can endure no more, remember to go to God. Let Him hide you in His presence for a while. Let Him fill those hurting places. Let Him wrap His arms around you and shelter you. Then, when you are ready, when you have found your place in Him once again, come out, and sing, "You are my refuge and my fortress, my God in whom I trust." (Psalm 91:2 GW)

> "He will cover you with his feathers, and under his wings you will find refuge. His truth is your shield and armor. (Psalm 91: 4) "May you receive a rich reward from the LORD God of

Israel, under whose protection you
have come for shelter." (Ruth 2:12 GW)

Psalm 62

66 I know you don't believe me, but it will get better."
These were words spoken to me when I was
near my lowest, when I felt hopeless and didn't want
to try anymore. Words. That's all they were. Yet these
words stirred both anger and hope. Anger because
this little whip of a nurse couldn't possibly understand what I felt and what I was dealing with. Hope
because the possibility that she might be right was
a thread to hang on to.

There are times in our life when we fret about
the next paycheck, food for the table, the troubled or
lost child, the unfaithful spouse, the family member
who refuses to see their need of a savior, the unset-
tling report from the doctor, and the pain that just
will never go away. We worry, we pray, we scream
and beg God to move mountains but don't see the
answers or results that we feel we should have. We
are so overwhelmed we cannot cope with even the
smallest of tasks. We fall into despair from which

there seems to be no relief. We start to lose hope. God is so much bigger than all of this.

HOPE. There is always hope.

> "Wait calmly for God alone, my soul, because my hope comes from him. He alone is my rock and my savior— my stronghold. I cannot be shaken. My salvation and my glory depend on God. God is the rock of my strength, my refuge. Trust him at all times, you people. Pour out your hearts in his presence. God is our refuge. *Selah*" (Psalm 62:5-8 GW)

Selah. Stop. Pause. Listen.

David understood hope. In the midst of being unjustly chased, his life in constant danger, and his motives questioned, he turned to God alone. I like how he tells himself to "wait calmly for God alone." Other translations put it this way: "wait in silence." David talks to himself and tells his soul to be quiet, be calm, and find God. Sometimes we just need to say, "Self, shut up and listen!" You can say it a little more poetically as David did if you like. But you get the point. Be quiet.

He goes on to list ten things he knows for sure about God. God is his rock, his savior, his strength, his refuge, and his salvation. God listens. His glory is and will be God's glory. God can be trusted. With God, he cannot be permanently shaken. And HOPE COMES FROM GOD.

Jesus spoke these words to the people who were so burdened by life and religious rules. "Come to me, all who are tired from carrying heavy loads, and I will give you rest. Place my yoke over your shoulders, and learn from me, because I am gentle and humble. Then you will find rest for yourselves because my yoke is easy and my burden is light." (Matthew 11:28-30 GW)

Jesus is capable of carrying all your troubles. He really truly does understand what you are dealing with. He knows the brokenness of your heart. He will provide at the right time in the right way. Just realize dear friend that it may not be what you expected, but it will always be what you needed.

> "Turn all your anxiety over to God because he cares for you. Keep your mind clear, and be alert. Your opponent the devil is prowling around like a roaring lion as he looks for someone to devour. Be firm in the faith and resist him, knowing that other

believers throughout the world are
going through the same kind of suffering. God, who shows you his kindness and who has called you through
Christ Jesus to his eternal glory, will
restore you, strengthen you, make you
strong, and support you as you suffer
for a little while. Power belongs to him
forever. Amen." (1 Peter 5:7-11 GW)

Psalm 66: Part One

I love music. I can't remember a time not being happy when singing, playing the piano, or listening to music. I well remember God providing my piano to worship Him with as an adult, a story for another time. From the day I became a Christ follower I have not stopped singing to Him. I came to know Him because of music. I have worshipped, cried, and listened to Him while sitting at my piano. Music is a major part of who I am in Christ. The Bible has much to say about music and its importance to praise and worship. Let's take a look together.

> "Shout happily to God, all the earth!
> Make music to praise the glory of his
> name. Make his praise glorious. Say
> to God, "How awe-inspiring are your
> deeds! Your power is so great that your
> enemies will cringe in front of you. The
> whole earth will worship you. It will
> make music to praise you. It will make

music to praise your name. S*elah*"
(Psalm 66:1-4 GW)

Selah. Stop. Pause. Listen.

God loves music. Stand on the shores of the ocean in the quiet darkness of night and listen to the waves roll and break on the shore. Stand there when the storm is raging and hear the deep thundering roar as the waves crash against the rocks moving sand and stone and debris with its force. Walk in the forest quietly and listen to the wind in the trees. Look up and see them sway, moving to the musical melody of heaven. Listen to the cry of the eagle, the chirp of the finch, the rhythmic hum of the humming-bird. Listen to the lone cry of the wolf and coyote. Sit quietly beside a creek as the water moves gently down its path. Hear the music of nature worshipping God, its creator. "Let them praise the name of the LORD because they were created by his command." (Psalm 148:5 GW)

God will be praised. All the earth, whether animal, human, land, or nation will someday worship God. Imagine that day when even those who have refused to acknowledge God will bow in submission before him and pay homage to his name.

> "Your power is so great that your
> enemies will cringe in front of you."
> (Psalm 66:3b GW)

Take time and listen to creation worshiping and praising God. Then let your praise and worship be heard as you are filled with his glory. "Shout happily to God, all the earth! Make music to praise the glory of his name. Make his praise glorious." (Psalm 66:1-2 GW)

> "You will live in joy and peace. The
> mountains and hills, the trees of the
> field—all the world around you—will
> rejoice." (Isaiah 55:12 TLB) "Let
> everything alive give praises to the
> Lord! *You* praise him! Hallelujah!"
> (Psalm 150:6 TLB)

Psalm 66: Part Two

G rowing up, the living room was a special room in the house that was not used often. If you were in the living room, it was a special occasion such as Christmas, a birthday, company, or slide night.

I loved slide night. Dad would get out the screen and slide projector, Mom would make popcorn. Boxes of slide filled trays would be pulled from the front closet. The screen was set up, projector leveled, lights turned out, and the show would begin.

Dad ran the projector. There were slides of their wedding, Dad's time in the military, a toddler picture of my brother wearing a cowboy hat and holding the toy pistol backwards, Christmases past, holidays at the shore, and so many more. Stories would be told as slides piqued curiosity, some funny, others just reminiscent. It was a special family night. It was history, our history. It bound us together as a family.

"Come and see what God has done—
his awe-inspiring deeds for Adam's

descendants. He turned the sea into dry land. They crossed the river on foot. We rejoiced because of what he did there. He rules forever with his might. His eyes watch the nations. Rebels will not be able to oppose him. *Selah*" (Psalm 66:5-7 GW)

Selah. Stop. Pause. Listen.

Do you see how the psalmist remembers God in his life? He calls these remembrances "awe-inspiring deeds". He remembers his nation's history with God, how God took care of them. He wrote it down, made it visual, kind of like having a photo today. It is something that he could hold up, point to, and say, "Remember when." I can envision him standing tall as he talks to others about God. "Do you remember when God did this?" "Do you remember our grandparents telling us how they walked across dry land between walls of water?" "Do you remember them telling us how this made them feel?"

He has his Selah moment. Because of his reminiscing he reminds himself and others that no one can stand against God. I can see the writer becoming confident and sure of God in his life. All doubts leave and his faith becomes strong.

Memories are important. You need to remember the times that God healed you, or provided for you, or intervened for you, or disciplined you and taught you. As you talk about your God memories, your faith, trust, and hope in God will grow. You will find yourself becoming more confident, strong, and courageous. "However, be careful, and watch yourselves closely so that you don't forget the things which you have seen with your own eyes. Don't let them fade from your memory as long as you live. Teach them to your children and grandchildren." (Deuteronomy 4:9 GW)

Take time to write down the things that God has done for you. Call it a journal, a diary, or a book. It doesn't matter. Maybe you have a picture or an object that reminds you of a time God spoke to you or loved on you. Share these with others to help and encourage them in their journey with God. Share your memories of God helping and teaching you. "Remember the miracles he performed, the amazing things he did and the judgments he pronounced." (1 Chronicles 16:12 GW)

> "I will remember the deeds of the Lord.
> I will remember your ancient mira-
> cles. I will reflect on all your actions
> and think about what you have done."
> (Psalm 77:11-12 GW)

Psalm 66: Part Three

I liked school. I got along well with many of my teachers in school because I kept their rules. I couldn't understand why anyone would break the rules. Even though I like following rules I was and still am an independent thinker. I don't always follow the crowd. I prefer researching for myself what I choose to believe. I have been told I wear my emotions on my sleeve which makes me a lousy liar because my face is so easy to read.

Growing up I can't remember being bad even though I was called the rebellious one of the family. When I lost my temper, which was frequent, it got ugly. There are some painful and some funny memories of my temper that I am certainly not proud of. I had many Anne Shirley moments in my younger years. Truth is I still do. I was and am a basically good person, but in God's kingdom that is not enough.

"I will offer you a sacrifice of fattened livestock for burnt offerings with the

smoke from rams. I will offer cattle
and goats. *Selah*" (Psalm 66:15 GW)

Selah. Stop. Pause. Listen.

This psalmist had a wonderful understanding of
God. And his psalm has been an amazing journey
through his worship experience. We read his ecstatic
soaring praise in verses 1-4, then his remembering
the past in verses 5-7. He shows his understanding
of how God uses trials and hardships to teach, grow,
and draw us to Him in verses 8-12. Finally, the cul-
mination of this praise and understanding is fulfilled
in his desire for the burnt offering in verses 13-15.

What was the meaning and purpose of the burnt
offering, why was it so important, and how does it
apply to us today?

The burnt offering was a sacrifice meant for the
forgiveness of sin and asking God for a renewed
relationship with Him. The offering was given twice
daily, weekly, monthly, and yearly with a few holidays
added in for good measure. It was non-stop. There
was always a burnt offering on the altar. The smell
of burning meat would have been a continuous pun-
gent odor in the air. Are you impressed yet with the
enormity of this sacrifice? Do you start to see the
impossibility of remaining sinless before God with
this method of atonement?

Can you imagine the personal cost to each individual? The writer of this psalm definitely had some wealth because he could afford cattle and goats for his burnt offerings. The poor were allowed doves for their sacrifice. Still, there was no amount of sacrificing whether rich or poor that could permanently erase sin from a person. There was no permanent solution to having a relationship with God.

Enter Jesus.

"No one else can save us. Indeed, we can be saved only by the power of the one named Jesus and not by any other person." (Acts 4:12 GW) There is not room enough to explain how Jesus was the ultimate burnt offering here. Suffice it to say that He was It. Because of Jesus, we do not need to continuously ask for forgiveness of sin. He did it. He took it. We can stand in God's presence because of Jesus and his sacrifice. "Yes, all have sinned; all fall short of God's glorious ideal; yet now God declares us "not guilty" of offending him if we trust in Jesus Christ, who in his kindness freely takes away our sins." (Romans 3:23-24 TLB) "God saved you through faith as an act of kindness. You had nothing to do with it. Being saved is a gift from God. It's not the result of anything you've done, so no one can brag about it." (Ephesians 2:8-9 GW)

"If you declare that Jesus is Lord, and believe that God brought him back to life, you will be saved. By believing you receive God's approval, and by declaring your faith you are saved. Scripture says, "Whoever believes in him will not be ashamed." (Romans 10:9-11 GW)

Psalm 67

There's nothing that can make us smile and lighten our day better than the laughter of an infant. When my daughter was about 6 months old, we were using a diaper service. They had a promotion for professional pictures done right in your home. We decided to take them up on it.

The day arrived and the photographer set up his equipment. My usually bright and sunny little girl clammed up and just wouldn't smile! She was intimidated by all the equipment and the stranger that was trying to get a good smile out of her. There was nothing I could do or say to get her to smile.

Daddy came to the rescue. He got behind the photographer and started his special game with her. He called her by name and jumped and made her favorite funny noises. Then it happened. The biggest grin came over her and filled not only her face but her whole little person. The session went off without a hitch.

When the salesman returned a few weeks later with the proofs, we were offered a free package if we would allow them to use her photo in their promotions. Of course, as proud parents, we said yes. That picture of her in her little red and white dress is still one of my most favorite pictures of her. The joy on her face lit up the room.

> "May God have pity on us and bless
> us! May he smile on us. *Selah*"
> (Psalm 67:1 GW)

Selah. Stop. Pause. Listen.

I like this verse! May He smile on us. I can see God's face so full of joy, wonder, and laughter when He is thinking about us. He loves you! God doesn't just feel sorry for you. No, His compassion for you goes to the point of His sharing your pain with you. He completely understands what you're going through. Then, with all compassion and grace He blesses you. In the midst of all the pain, all the sorrow, all the confusion, He blesses you and His face lights up because of you.

Why is this so important? The next Selah says it all, "Then your ways will be known on earth, your salvation throughout all nations. Let everyone give thanks to you, O God. Let everyone give thanks to you.

Let the nations be glad and sing joyfully because you judge everyone with justice and guide the nations on the earth. *Selah*" (Psalm 67:2-4 GW)

Selah. Stop. Pause. Listen.

Remember Job? God was so proud of him, so sure of him that he let Satan test him. God knew the whole time what Job was going through. Job struggled and questioned in the midst of unimaginable physical, emotional, and mental pain. He lost wealth, children, and health. All he had left was a wife who encouraged him to curse God and friends that applied their own brand of logic to his pain. He refused to blame God, but he did ask why. He begged for understanding.

Through all this, God continued to have compassion on Job. He continued to show grace and love to Job. It's hard to understand that God actually smiled on him as He watched him go through these difficulties. And when it was all over, He gave back to Job even more than before.

What if instead of thinking "why me Lord?" when going through difficult times, you think "why not me Lord?" Your pain and suffering are what God is using to show Himself to the world. This doesn't mean that you have to be joyful at this time. Please feel all the pain, all the anger, all the frustrations and hurts that are coming your way. Take all the time you need to process this devastating time. Know this though; you aren't alone in what you're going through. God's grace and compassion are surrounding you. Know that God is walking with you through this season of life even if you don't feel Him.

Sometimes blessings really are hidden in pains, blessings that will show the world the God they so desperately need.

> "Consider it a sheer gift, friends, when tests and challenges come at you from all sides. You know that under pressure, your faith-life is forced into the open and shows its true colors. So don't try to get out of anything prematurely. Let it do its work so you become mature and well-developed, not deficient in any way." (James 1:2-4 MSG)

Psalm 68: Part One

In my youth I had the pleasure of being part of a
few parades. I got to be a clown in one of them.
It was a warm summer day as we marched down
the parade route through town waving to bystanders,
tossing candy to children, and just plain having fun.
My high school band was always a part of the Macy's
Day Thanksgiving parade and the St. Patrick's Day
parade in New York City. I wasn't part of the band, but
I always watched the parade on TV waiting to cheer
for our local band as they marched past the cameras.

It was just as exciting to watch a parade in person.
I remember waiting on the side of the road with antic-
ipation listening for the approach of the first band
and the Grand Marshall. As the Grand Marshall,
usually a local dignitary or famous person came
into view, the excitement mounted. The parade had
officially begun. The youngest in the crowd would
start to jump and point. Bands, decorated floats, and
people dressed in costumes would parade past us.
Oohs and aahs and laughter would be heard as we

pointed at the sight before us, trying not to miss all the exciting moments. Who doesn't like a parade?

> "O God, when you went in front of your people, when you marched through the desert, *Selah"* (Psalm 68:7 GW)

Selah. Stop. Pause. Listen.

Psalm 68 is a wonderful psalm of encouragement, remembrance, and worship. I like the opening phrase, "God will arise." (Psalm 68:1GW) Then the closing verse "God, the God of Israel, is awe-inspiring in his holy place. He gives strength and power to his people. Thanks be to God!" (Psalm 68:35 GW) Each Selah has so much to say that I think we should spend some time looking at each one on its own. Today, let's look at the first of the three Selahs of this psalm.

We often refer to Israel's time in the desert as wandering. We think of purposeless wandering due to their inability to trust God about taking the Promised Land. It stands like a beacon before us, warning us not to do the same. But what if God actually orchestrated the whole forty years? How would your perspective change if, instead of envisioning aimless wandering, you see a well-crafted plan?

God was not unaware of their lack of faith. It would have been wonderful if they had that faith and trust and could march right into the land. But God knew they would need the desert. God knew they would need time before they could step out in faith with Him. As Israel moved throughout the wilderness, God was in front leading them.

In this desert place, God taught Israel to know Him. He provided manna and quail when they were hungry, water when they were thirsty. He taught them to move when He moved and stay when He stayed. He taught them to hear His voice. He taught them follow. God was leading, teaching, training. They learned to be a nation. They learned to be set apart, to be different from all those around them. They ultimately learned to trust God so that when He said go, they went.

So, when you feel that you are once again wandering aimlessly through your life filled with fear and doubt, remember Israel in the wilderness. God really is leading you through your wilderness. He really does have a plan for you at this time. He is in front of you like a Grand Marshall in all His glory, protecting you, teaching you and strengthening you. And when your wandering is done, ...

> "You will go out with joy and be led out
> in peace. The mountains and the hills

will break into songs of joy in your presence, and all the trees will clap their hands." (Isaiah 55:12 GW)

Psalm 68: Part Two

"Thanks be to the Lord, who daily carries our burdens for us. God is our salvation. *Selah*" (Psalm 68:19)

Selah. Stop. Pause. Listen.

I have to admit that I've struggled to explain this verse, even for myself. It smacks of the hollow platitudes that well-meaning friends, family, and believers said to ease their own discomfort when I was in desperate pain. How often in my life have I panicked, fought, manipulated, and bargained with God over issues that He simply wanted to carry for me? How much easier and peaceful my life with Him would have been, and still could be, if I would just let Him carry these burdens as He promised. Yet, I fight, I give and take back. I think that I have totally surrendered only to realize that once again I have taken control.

And there it is: control. I want to be in control. It comes down to trust, doesn't it? Do I believe what He says?

Burdens come in many shapes and sizes. Failures, past and present, real or perceived; children that are struggling into adulthood; job loss, job change, finances; sickness, whether temporary, chronic, or life threatening — the list goes on. Though we say we trust God, somehow, we feel that it is our responsibility to carry this weight through life.

It's like standing knee deep in the middle of a huge mud puddle with that mucky ooze slowly creeping up and through you. Instead of stepping out into His waiting arms, you try on your own to get out, only getting more covered in that awful mud. If you just reached for God's hand, He would help you out. The mud puddle would still be there, but now you will have the ability to view it from God's perspective and see His plan for it.

Salvation in this verse is not just about forgiveness of sins; it is about protection from harm, ruin, and loss. It is like a bridge that God builds over the muddy mess. God could choose to instantly dry up that loathsome puddle and make it look like it was never there. But more likely the puddle will stay. God will build a bridge over it. Together, you will walk over this puddle and view the mess from a safe vantage point on His Bridge, clean and dry, until you reach the other side.

God knows your struggle. God desires to protect you, help you, and care for you. Let Him build his bridge of protection for you and then, with Him, you can walk over your puddle. "Your God has decided you will be strong." (Psalm 68:28a GW)

> "Turn all your anxiety over to God because he cares for you." (1 Peter 5:7 GW)

Psalm 68: Part Three

What comes to mind when you think of worship? For some it's visions of faces turned heavenward with arms lifted high. Others see people kneeling with heads bowed and hands clasped in prayer. Some believe that worship only occurs within the walls of a church. Maybe for you it is a walk through the woods or sitting by a lake and talking with God. Maybe, like me, you sit at the piano and let music, whether already written or just made up, flow through your hands and heart. Others see worship as the actions they do by serving God in soup kitchens or on the mission field. These are all forms of worship. One isn't more holy or more right than the other.

> "You kingdoms of the world, sing to God. Make music to praise the Lord. *Selah*" (Psalm 68:32 GW)

Selah. Stop. Pause. Listen.

Throughout this psalm David showed God as protector, warrior, savior, teacher, powerful, and holy. With this final Selah of Psalm 68, David invites us all to worship God.

But what is worship? Is worship some ethereal experience of awe? Is there a right and wrong way to worship? Since we are to worship, how, when, and where should it be done? Worship is not that hard. Let's take a look.

Simply put, worship is a lifestyle. It is constant. It encompasses all we do, all that we say, and how we live. There is no one way that is more worshipful than another. Worship is about one thing and only one thing. It is about God. Worship honors God's sovereignty and holiness. Worship deepens our walk with God and interacts with every part of our lives. Worship comes from the heart. It is pure and truthful. It has no plans of honoring self, only honoring God. We worship when we pray, study the Bible, attend church, sing, dance, go fishing, work, play, and so much more. Worship is an act of the heart.

We worship because we know He loves us. We worship because in spite of all our failures and all our misfortunes in life, He still loves us. We worship because He leads us through our wildernesses. We worship because He carries all our burdens. We worship because He is. We worship, not because we have it all together, but because we don't.

David murdered a man and stole his wife. He was a fighter and at times ruthless. He worshipped God. Samuel, a prophet called by God at a young age and highly respected, had children who didn't follow in his footsteps. He worshipped God. A woman, known only as a sinner, washed Jesus' feet with her tears, wiped them with her hair, and anointed them. She worshipped God. Jonah ran from God and ended in the belly of a large fish. He worshipped God. Abraham lied about his wife and tried to circumvent God's plan for an heir. He worshipped God. Peter, ever impulsive, struggled to learn to think before acting or speaking and made many mistakes. He worshipped God. "God, the God of Israel, is awe-inspiring in his holy place. He gives strength and power to his people. Thanks be to God!" (Psalm 68:35 GW)

> "Brothers and sisters, in view of all we have just shared about God's compassion, I encourage you to offer your bodies as living sacrifices, dedicated to God and pleasing to him. This kind of worship is appropriate for you. Don't become like the people of this world. Instead, change the way you think. Then you will always be able

to determine what God really wants—
what is good, pleasing, and perfect."
(Romans 12:1-2 GW)

Psalm 75

I n eighth grade, I was given a job of great responsibility. I was chosen from a class of about 300
students to be one of a dozen hall monitors. Being
a hall monitor meant that I got to spend my day at
a desk in one of the hallways. To have this position
required me to be an excellent student, trustworthy,
and able to study independently. I had to be watchful.

When it was my turn to be front hall monitor, I sat
at a desk in the foyer next to the office watching who
came in and out of the building. While there I got
to run errands for the office such as deliver papers
to the various classrooms or escort students to the
office. As a back hall monitor my desk was at the
back entrance next to the washrooms. The back hall
was my favorite since it was quiet and undisturbed.

My day of testing as hall monitor came, bringing
with it emotions of overwhelming fear and amazing
courage. It was recess and classes were going in
and out the rear entrance. I was at my desk working
on a drawing of the human body's muscular system.

One student, who was known to be a bully, came bursting into the hall from outside to use the washroom. I don't know what he was angry about, but I watched, wide eyed, as he kicked a hole in the door. He looked at me and me at him. Panic rose like a flag hoisted. With threats of retaliation if I told anyone, he marched out of the building.

I sat there, frozen to my seat. I realized I had a decision to make. Either I trusted his threats and lied to the principal about how the door got busted, or I went to the principal, told the truth, and let the pieces land where they may. I chose the latter. The truth and my place of trust were more important than the fear of being bullied.

Full of fear and trembling from head to toe, I walked to the office. I told what happened and who did it. The principal went out to the field and brought in the offender straight to my desk there in the hall. I confirmed that this bully was the culprit. As the principal took him by the arm, he looked back at me muttering threats of retaliation. He never did follow through.

That day I discovered courage in the face of fear. I learned about the consequences of good and bad. I learned the value of standing apart from the group.

Asaph wrote psalm 75 to teach about good versus evil and God's timing concerning both. He heard the voice of God speak to him, "God says, "At the time I have planned, I will bring justice against the wicked. When the earth quakes and its people live in turmoil, I am the one who keeps its foundations firm. *Interlude*" (Psalm 75:2-3 NLT)

Selah. Stop. Pause. Listen.

For the Christ follower the world today seems to be spinning out of control at lightning speed. We see what is morally wrong being declared as right and we are called intolerant or worse if we don't agree. Our unwavering faith in God and His principles are challenged on a near daily basis, and we feel as if we are quickly losing moral ground. Yet we stand as a beacon of light in a world going dark while we have the bully staring in our face uttering threats of retaliation.

Asaph also struggled in a world that wasn't interested in God or His principles. I'm sure that he cried out in prayer for justice. This is what he learned. "For no one on earth—from east or west, or even from the wilderness should raise a defiant fist. It is God alone who judges; he decides who will rise and who will fall." (Psalm 75:6-7 NLT) This is how Paul put it when writing to the Ephesians. "This is not a wrestling match against a human opponent. We are wrestling with rulers, authorities, the powers who govern this world of darkness, and spiritual forces that control evil in the heavenly world. For this reason, take up all the armor that God supplies. Then you will be able to take a stand during these evil days. Once you have overcome all obstacles, you will be able to stand your ground." (Ephesians 6:12-13 GW)

We are called to stand firm and it is unwavering trust in God that keeps us firmly rooted. According to scripture, we can't stop the moral decay of the world around us. It's part of God's plan. But we can stand as a beacon of light. We can set our moral compass on God and leave Him to judge in His time and his way. As He says, "I will destroy all the weapons of wicked people, but the weapons of righteous people will be raised proudly." (Psalm 75:10 GW)

Revelation has this to say about the final judgement. "I saw a large, white throne and the one who was sitting on it. The earth and the sky fled from his presence, but no place was found for them. I saw the dead, both important and unimportant people, standing in front of the throne. Books were opened, including the Book of Life. The dead were judged on the basis of what they had done, as recorded in the books. The sea gave up its dead. Death and hell gave up their dead. People were judged based on what they had done. Death and hell were thrown into the fiery lake. (The fiery lake is the second death.) Those whose names were not found in the Book of

Life were thrown into the fiery lake." (Revelation 20:11-15 GW)

Like Asaph we can rejoice. He never stopped praising God or testifying about His miracles. Neither should we. We can shout our praises to God from every rooftop to all who will listen. God wins. And we win if we keep ourselves firmly planted in Him.

> "Then Jesus said to them, "So wherever you go in the world, tell everyone the Good News. Whoever believes and is baptized will be saved, but whoever does not believe will be condemned." (Mark 16:15-16 GW)

Psalm 76

I had followed God from the age of thirteen. I was a good girl. I didn't break the rules nor bend them. I didn't get into drugs, alcohol, or mischief. I did struggle with an unruly temper though. I attended church, seldom missing a Sunday. I tithed; I was on the worship team. As an adult, I was a missionary and pastor's wife.

But I was getting divorced. How had this happened? What was I supposed to do now? I had honored God from a young age and now my perfect world was crashing down around me.

I stayed with some friends who were our accountability partners. There I prayed, looking for answers. Two mornings in a row, I woke with a book, chapter, and verse on my mind. This is the only time in my life that this happened. As I shared those verses with my friends, we agreed that God was leading me on a very unexpected path. I was on a journey, and He would be with me through it.

I returned to my childhood home, broken, scared, and destitute. God provided a church that had a ministry of restoration to the broken. I was right where God wanted me. Slowly He restored me. I became stronger and confident. Because of this time, I know God in a way that I never have before.

Psalm 76 was penned by Asaph sometime after Sennacherib, king of Assyria, attacked Judah. You can read this account in Isaiah 37. This psalm is Asaph's interpretation of the event, his teaching about God and then he writes a prophetic word about the coming of Jesus.

Hezekiah, a king who chose whole heartedly to follow God, reopened the temple, destroyed all the places of idol worship within Judah, and befriended Isaiah. He wanted Judah restored to God. When Sennacherib showed up to take Judah into captivity, Hezekiah ran to God. He went straight to the temple and prayed. That night God killed 185,000 soldiers in Sennacherib's army. No fighting, no noise, just dead bodies everywhere the next morning.

> "God is known in Judah. His name is great in Israel. His tent is in Salem. His home is in Zion. There he destroyed flaming arrows, shields, swords, and weapons of war. *Selah*"
> (Psalm 76:1-3 GW)

Selah. Stop. Pause. Listen.

The names Judah, Israel, Salem, and Zion really caught my attention. Asaph was making a point with them. Let's look at the meaning of each of these places. Judah means praise; Israel, God Prevails; Salem, peace; and Zion, a parched place that became the symbol of God's presence and joy. What is Asaph saying then?

God loves your dry, desert places. There He lives with you and turns that desert into a place of joy. You learn to rely on God in a way that only happens because of the desert. There, in the desert, God wins. He always wins. What Satan meant as destruction, God will and has redeemed and turned to joy.

> "You alone must be feared! Who can stand in your presence when you become angry? From heaven you announced a verdict. The earth was fearful and silent when you rose to judge, O God when you rose to save every oppressed person on earth. *Selah*" (Psalm 76:7-9 GW)

Selah. Stop. Pause. Listen.

Remember, God destroyed everything that Sennacherib brought against Judah. Knowing that, Asaph is not saying that you need to be afraid of God in the sense of the shaking in your boots meaning of fear. Rather, fear in this verse means honor, respect, and awe. Look at what God accomplished when Hezekiah earnestly prayed. He respected God. He knew that only God would have the answer to the problem.

When you were in difficult times and God intervened, weren't you amazed at the outcome? There is no need to be afraid of God. Instead, you can "... go confidently to the throne of God's kindness to receive mercy and find kindness, which will help us at the right time." (Hebrews 4:16 GW)

I love the word 'save' in verse 9. It means to victoriously liberate from moral troubles.

This is the prophetic look ahead to the coming of Jesus. God wants a relationship with you. To do that, He made a decision. Jesus would come and Satan was shaking in his boots! Jesus doesn't just get rid of a few problems, He liberates you. Total freedom! Sin no longer controls you. "He is the payment for our sins, and not only for our sins, but also for the sins of the whole world." (1 John 2:2 GW)

Jesus has liberated you. That doesn't mean that bad things won't happen or that you won't struggle at times. But when it does happen, run to your meeting place with Jesus. There, lay out the problem before Him. There, in that dry, troublesome place, praise Him and watch Him destroy the enemy of your soul and liberate you. Don't we have an awesome God?

> "Stand still, and see what the LORD will do to save you today. The LORD is fighting for you! So be still!" (Exodus 14:13a, 14 GW)

Psalm 77

I remember the tears that wouldn't stop and the embarrassment at having come to such a place. I was broken. Life as I'd known it was over. Why was I here? Why me, Lord? Would God ever release me from this place of horrible pain? I felt doomed to endless misery. It was the dark night of my soul. The only prayer left was "Why, God?" I hung on because I didn't know what else to do.

Asaph cried the same prayer. "Loudly, I cried to God. Loudly, I cried to God so that he would open his ears to hear me. On the day I was in trouble, I went to the Lord for help. At night I stretched out my hands in prayer without growing tired. Yet, my soul refused to be comforted. I sigh as I remember God. I begin to lose hope as I think about him. *Selah*" (Psalm 77:1-3 GW)

Selah. Stop. Pause. Listen.

The pain never ends. God seems so distant and far away. Earnest prayers seem to go unanswered. The feeling that God doesn't care nags at your hurting soul. You remember the days of laughter with longing and hopelessness.

Pain may be universal, but to you it's personal. No one truly knows what you're feeling, what you're going through. Agonizing pain of the heart is the one walk that you take alone. You'll be okay. But for now, you're on a journey.

Along the journey of his dark night Asaph asked six questions. These questions weren't directed at God. They were directed to his soul.

"Will the LORD reject me for all time?

Will he ever accept me?

Has his mercy come to an end forever?

Has his promise been canceled throughout every generation?

Has God forgotten to be merciful?

Has he locked up his compassion because of his anger? *Selah*" (Psalm 77:7-9 GW)

Selah. Stop. Pause. Listen.

I think that as we go through our dark night, each of us has asked these questions in one form or another. These questions aren't looking for answers, they are making statements. God hasn't rejected you. He always accepts you. His promise for you is real and hasn't changed. God is merciful, always. He's not angry at you or compassionless. Ask the question, know the truth.

After asking this series of rhetorical questions, Asaph made a decision. He would start to worship. He looked to the past. He remembered the good days and how God was there. "I will remember the deeds of the LORD. I will remember your ancient miracles. I will reflect on all your actions and think about what you have done. O God, your ways are holy! What god is as great as our God? You are the God who performs miracles. You have made your strength known among the nations. With your might you have defended your people, the descendants of Jacob and Joseph. *Selah*" (Psalm 77:11-15 GW)

Selah. Stop. Pause. Listen.

Remember the times when God provided for you. Remember the times when God intervened for you. Remember the joy of the day when you turned your life over to God and received His wonderful gift of salvation. Remember the days of laughter and joy. Remember.

Asaph described the road of grief well. "Your road went through the sea. Your path went through raging water, but your footprints could not be seen. Like a shepherd, you led your people. You had Moses and Aaron take them by the hand." (Psalm 77:19-20 GW)

Your grief is your own and no one can tell you how long it will take. For some it's days, for others it's years. Like Asaph and many others before you, you will get through it. Take your time, ask your questions, and dig deep into God. God hasn't abandoned you. God is close beside you and at times, He will carry you. God knows, He really does.

> "Don't be afraid, because I am with you.
> Don't be intimidated; I am your God.
> I will strengthen you. I will help you.
> I will support you with my victorious
> right hand." (Isaiah 41:10 GW)

Psalm 81

After much praising and begging, my friend finally shared her recipe with me. I was elated! I followed the recipe, eager to share this confection with my family. I changed it just a little though. It called for toffee chips and pecans, but I used chocolate chips and raisins because that's what I had. She used softened butter, but I substituted cheap oil. I cut the amount of sugar in half. I was supposed to add the liquids a little at a time, I just dumped it all in. The egg whites needed to be beaten to soft peaks and slowly folded in. I thought it would be okay to just dump the eggs in with the liquids, it's faster that way. Bake slowly, but faster is better.

I was so disappointed when I pulled this delicacy from the oven. It didn't taste or look the same. I was sure that she was hiding some very important ingredient or step from me. Why would she do this to me? I thought we were good friends. I guess she really wanted to keep the family recipe all in the family. I would never make it again. Why try? It would never be as good as hers.

I wouldn't admit for a long time that the failure was mine. I wanted to blame her. We are still friends. I now follow her recipe to the letter, making no substitutions, and it turns out perfectly every time.

Psalm 87 shows us what life could be if we would just follow God His way. But it also shows what life will be if we choose to continue to walk in our own brand of Christianity by making our own rules.

> "I heard a message I did not understand: "When you were in trouble, you called out to me, and I rescued you. I was hidden in thunder, but I answered you. I tested your loyalty at the oasis of Meribah. *Selah*" (Psalm 81:5b-7 GW)

Selah. Stop. Pause. Listen.

There is a lot in this one Selah. God spoke with Asaph a message to be shared with Israel. God wanted Israel to remember what He did for them. He had brought them out of Egypt, freeing them from slavery. They saw the plagues decimate Egypt. They saw the Red Sea parted and then walked through it dry as a bone. They watched as God destroyed the army of Egypt by drowning them. God proved His power and protection. When they needed help, He answered.

And then there was Meribah. They were thirsty. After all that God had just done, they complained and blamed God because of no water. They wouldn't trust God to provide for them. Instead, they continued to question God's ability to provide and grumbled against God. "This was the oasis of Meribah [Complaining], where the Israelites complained about the LORD and where he showed them he was holy." (Numbers 20:13 GW) God once again proved Himself to them. He miraculously gave them water but at a cost.

What follows in this psalm is quite sad. "Listen, my people, and I will warn you. Israel, if you would only listen to me! But my people did not listen to me. Israel wanted nothing to do with me. So I let them go their own stubborn ways and follow their own advice." (Verses 8, 11-12 GW) The books of Judges, Samuel, Kings, and Chronicles, tells the hardships and losses that Israel suffered because of their continued disobedience and lack of trust. There are a few good accounts but, in the end, Israel lost their country and went into exile. It would be a long time before God would open the way for them to return and start again.

What can you learn from this psalm? You have a choice. You can follow God according to His ways or you can be stubborn, picking and choosing your own rules for following God. "So I let them go their own stubborn ways and follow their own advice." (Psalm 8:12 GW)

God redeemed you, set you free from the power and control of sin over you through the death and resurrection of Jesus. With that you now have an obligation to live a life of trust and obedience for God according to His ways. "You were slaves to sin. But I thank God that you have become wholeheartedly obedient to the teachings which you were given. Freed from sin, you were made slaves who do what God approves of." (Romans 6:17-18 GW)

I am not talking about legalism that is just a change on the outside with no change in the heart. You can't perform a list of do's and don't's thinking these make you a Christian. No, obedience comes from the heart. It is a desire to please and do what is right before God even when no one is looking.

God desires to protect you, support you, encourage you, grow you, and provide for you. God wants to walk with you. "So if you faithfully obey the commands I am giving you today—to love the LORD your God and to serve him with all your heart and with all your soul—then I will send rain on your land in its season, both autumn and spring rains, so that you may gather in your grain, new wine and olive oil. I will provide grass in the fields for your cattle, and you will eat and be satisfied. (Deuteronomy 11:13-15 NIV)

God gives us a wonderful promise in the last verses of this psalm if we obey. I encourage you to read for yourself. God promises that if you follow Him without question, He will defeat all your enemies and He will provide the best for you, even turning your trials into victories. Do not follow, and you will suffer life at your own hands. Which do you choose?

> "My dear friends, you have always obeyed, not only when I was with you but even more now that I'm absent. In the same way continue to work out your salvation with fear and trembling. It is God who produces in you the desires and actions that please him." (Philippians 2:12-13 GW)

Psalm 82

"How long are you going to judge unfairly? How long are you going to side with wicked people? *Selah*" (Psalm 82:2 GW)

Selah. Stop. Pause. Listen.

Judgement; it's both sobering and controversial. Though this psalm is directed at the leaders of Asaph's day, there is much that those of us who aren't officially in leadership can learn.

When justice is corrupted "all the foundations of the earth shake." (Psalm 82:5 GW) "Do you rulers really give fair verdicts? Do you judge Adam's descendants fairly? No, you invent new crimes on earth, and your hands spread violence." (Psalm 58:1-2 GW) Corruption in justice is nothing new. It's been around since the Fall of Man. None of us like to think about it, until we are faced with the reality of it. We will make a lot of noise especially if we think we've been unfairly treated.

Let's back up one verse. "God takes his place in his own assembly. He pronounces judgment among the gods:" (Psalm 82:1 GW)

The gods referred to in this verse are us humans. No, we aren't gods in the way that God is, we don't have special powers. Jesus quotes verse 6 of this psalm when talking with the religious leaders in John. "Jesus said to them, "Don't your Scriptures say, 'I said, "You are gods"'? The Scriptures cannot be discredited. So if God calls people gods (and they are the people to whom he gave the Scriptures), why do you say that I'm dishonoring God because I said, 'I'm the Son of God'?" (John 10:34-36 GW)

In John 10:22-42 Jesus called out the corruption of the religious leaders and they didn't like it. Sadly, the leaders were so concerned with making their lives comfortable at the expense of the people that they missed God in their midst.

Right now, God is standing in your midst ready to decide how well you judge. "Stop judging by outward appearance! Instead, judge correctly." (John 7:24 GW) There is a right way and a wrong way to do this.

You're called to judge rightly and fairly based on God's laws. In order to do this, you must first have knowledge of God's laws. You don't need a degree in biblical studies, but you do need to study the Bible regularly and prayerfully. You must surround yourself with other Christ followers to talk with and learn from. You must guard against developing your own ideas of right and wrong by letting the world and its corruption seep into your thinking. You can't pick and choose which of God's laws to follow, or worse, change them to suit your idea of justice. And with this knowledge, remember compassion. Always compassion.

"Do what God's word says. Don't merely listen to it, or you will fool yourselves. If someone listens to God's word but doesn't do what it says, he is like a person who looks at his face in a mirror, studies his features, goes away, and immediately forgets what he looks like. However, the person who continues to study God's perfect laws that make people free and who remains committed to them will be blessed. People like that don't merely listen and forget; they actually do what God's laws say." (James 1:22-25 GW) "Defend weak people and orphans. Protect the rights of the oppressed and the poor. Rescue weak and needy people. Help them escape the power of wicked people." (Psalm 82:3-4 GW)

Today it's becoming harder to see true justice as the line between good and evil becomes blurred. You are called to stand as a beacon of light and hope and justice to a lost and dying world. There will come a day when you will have to decide if you will stand firm against or bend to the subtle corruptions against God. I hope you choose to stand firm.

>"Righteous people will rejoice when they see God take revenge. They will wash their feet in the blood of wicked people. Then people will say, "Righteous people certainly have a reward. There is a God who judges on earth."" (Psalm 58:10-11 GW)

Psalm 83

The two years that I lived in a small Minnesota town there were a few tornados. I heard how the year before we arrived one passed very close to the town we lived in. That same year another one had gone through a nearby town destroying every home. The summer we sold our home on the lake and moved away, one touched down taking off our neighbor's roof and relocating more than a few docks and boats around the lake. It felt like the storms always went from watch to warning to sighting. The sky would turn an ominous grey-green. Then the clouds would start to roll around like a tangled pile of snakes. Lightning, rain, and hail were part of the storm. Then, if an eerie stillness came, look for the funnel.

I lived in fear of those storms. They were unpredictable and could be devastating in power. Fearing for my children's safety, I became a sky watcher. I wanted to protect them from the impending disasters.

I knew that only God could ultimately protect, but I would continue to be diligent in my watching.

The day is coming. We don't know when, but it is coming.

Selah. Stop. Pause. Listen.

Psalm 83 moves at the speed of an impending tornado. One verse flows to the next tying all together into two thoughts, the rant and the truth. I would encourage you to take a moment to read this psalm in its entirety to get the full benefit of this devotional.

Verses 1-8 are Asaph's cry to God about what the nations are planning to do to Israel. They are an arrogant lot. They are ganging up, making secret plans and backroom alliances. Asaph isn't fearful here. He is just saying, "Hey God! Do you see what they're doing? The nerve! They think they're all that and more! How dare they come after God's chosen!" When the rant is over Asaph breathes "*Selah*"

Selah. Stop. Pause. Listen.

Like Israel in Asaph's day, being a Christ follower sets you apart from the rest of the world. Co-workers, family members, and the person behind the counter are all watching you because you follow God.

"They make plans in secret against your people and plot together against those you treasure. They say, "Let's wipe out their nation so that the name of Israel will no longer be remembered."" (Psalm 83:3-4 GW) There is coming a day when to be a Christ follower will mean persecution and suffering. It already is for those in many other countries around the globe. Jesus said, "Everyone will hate you because of me, but the one who stands firm to the end will be saved." (Mark 13:13 NIV)

Asaph's second dialogue with God in verses 9-18 is encouraging. He reminds God of what He did to other nations and people who came against God's anointed. God protected and fought for Israel. Asaph knew that God will fight for them. He is saying, "Sic 'em God! I know you have, I know you will. Won't they be sorry when they come face to face with you!" "Let them be put to shame and terrified forever. Let them die in disgrace so that they must acknowledge you. Your name is the LORD. You alone are the Most High God of the whole earth." (Psalm 83:17-18GW)

God will fight for us. And we will go through persecution. We have been spared much of this in this nation and lifetime. I believe that more and more we will see our freedoms to worship strangled in North America. Take a moment to think about that.

Selah. Stop. Pause. Listen.

What would it mean to you to have all your religious freedoms taken away? Do you follow God only because it is convenient right now? Would you give in to demands to avoid discomfort, or will you stand firm for God? The Bible tells us about the end of time and the persecution of the saints.

"You must understand this: In the last days there will be violent periods of time. People will be selfish and love money. They will brag, be arrogant, and use abusive language. They will curse their parents, show no gratitude, have no respect for what is holy, and lack normal affection for their families. They will refuse to make peace with anyone. They will be slanderous, lack self-control, be brutal, and have no love for what is good. They will be traitors. They will be reckless and conceited. They will love pleasure rather than God. They will appear to have a godly life, but they will not let its power change them." (2 Timothy 3:1-5a GW)

Like Asaph we know that we are not the target, God is. Will you stand with God? Determine in your heart now who you will serve!

> "Behold, I (Jesus) am coming quickly,
> and My reward is with Me, to give to
> each one according to the merit of his

deeds (earthly works, faithfulness).I am the Alpha and the Omega, the First and the Last, the Beginning and the End [the Eternal One]." (Revelation 22:12-14 AMP)

Psalm 84

"Stay with Me." God was calling me to spend a special time with Him. I gathered a blanket, pillow, my Bible, some music, and went to the church and locked the door behind me. I spent the next five days in the church, just me and God. I made my bed at the altar. An incredible peace descended on the sanctuary during that stay.

In the early morning hours of the fifth day God called, "Come dance with me." I had just put the last big bite of a blueberry muffin in my mouth.

"But God, my teeth aren't brushed. My hair's a mess. I don't have any make-up on. I can't swallow this muffin! I'm not ready!"

Again, the call, "You are beautiful to me. Come dance with me."

His voice spoke gently, quietly calling me forward. His voice brought a longing, a peace, and joy all at once. I was about to dance with God. As I walked up the aisle, His presence met me and together we danced a dance that was meant only for the two of us. I was at peace as I danced with the One Who Intimately Loves Me. I had been to the Holy Place. My life was forever changed after that encounter.

> "Blessed are those who live in your house. They are always praising you. *Selah*" (Psalm 84:4 GW)

Selah. Stop. Pause. Listen.

Psalm 84 is commonly referred to as the psalm of peace. As you read it, there is a quietness that seems to naturally come over you. You can feel the peace, the strength the calm assurance that the writer felt.

The psalmist is longing heart, soul, and body for the place of constantly being in God's presence and the peace and joy that is found there. In verse 2 he expresses his hunger for this place to be like that of an infant crying to be fed. Nothing else will satisfy. He sees sparrows and swallows that have made nests in the temple. Free of life's distractions and problems, pain and suffering, the only thing left to do would be to praise and worship. Like him, I envy being in such a sequestered place with God.

This psalm is not about escaping the world though. Rather it's about finding that place of quiet solitude, just you and God, and while there, gaining strength to face the world and life's battles. "Blessed are those whose strength is in you, whose hearts are set on pilgrimage. As they pass through the Valley of Baka, they make it a place of springs;" (Psalm 84:5-6 NIV)

The Valley of Baka was a place of weeping or tears. David called it the Valley of Death in Psalm 23. You will go through hardships at some time in your life. You may even go through them more than once. But, when you have spent time, sitting, soaking, and learning in the presence of God, He will give you the strength to endure and come out. "I can guarantee this truth: You will cry because you are sad, but the world will be happy. You will feel pain, but your pain will turn to happiness." (John 16:20GW)

> "O LORD God, commander of armies,
> hear my prayer. Open your ears, O God
> of Jacob. *Selah*" (Psalm 84:8 GW)

Selah. Stop. Pause. Listen.

After spending time listening, watching, resting, and gaining strength from God's presence, the psalmist is now ready to pray. I like how he addresses God. He chooses his words carefully here. He calls Him Lord God, Commander of armies, and God of Jacob. When he calls Him Lord God he acknowledges God's sovereignty. As Commander of Armies,

He is our leader and defender. As God of Jacob, He is our comforter, and hope.

When you pray, know God. God has many names and that is a whole study in itself. Do you need a protector, teacher, defender, provider, comforter, friend, or father? God is all that and more.

And when you pray, take time to listen. Learn to Selah in your prayers. Learn to stop and pause and listen for what the Holy Spirit wants to say to you to comfort you and lead you. "Don't fret or worry. Instead of worrying, pray. Let petitions and praises shape your worries into prayers, letting God know your concerns. Before you know it, a sense of God's wholeness, everything coming together for good, will come and settle you down. It's wonderful what happens when Christ displaces worry at the center of your life." (Philippians 4:6-7 MSG)

> "LORD Almighty, blessed is the one
> who trusts in you." (Psalm 84:12 NIV)

Psalm 85

Somehow I knew from a young age that God was real and approachable. Not raised in a church-going home, I just didn't know how to find Him. I simply wanted to talk with God.

When I was 13, I was invited to a coffee house meeting that was held in the basement of a local church. My piano teacher who was there explained that if I confessed my sin and accepted Jesus as my Savior then I could talk with God. Bingo! Yes! If that's what it took to talk with God, I was in. Now I could have endless conversations with God!

Word quickly spread that another lost soul had been found. With congratulations and welcomes I was asked how I felt. I didn't know how to answer because I honestly didn't know. Someone took me aside and told me that I was supposed to feel happy now. For the rest of the evening, I said I felt happy. Actually, I was in a daze. I needed time to process this decision.

I returned the next week and continued going for many years. I was birthed into a community focused on worship and prayer. Friday nights found me sitting on the floor of the church basement joined with other youth singing worship songs followed by prayer in the upper prayer room praying till after midnight. I knew nothing else. I loved the presence of God that was so evident there. Not only did I talk with God in those meetings, but I also could talk with God whenever I wanted, wherever I wanted.

> "You removed your people's guilt.
> You pardoned all their sins. *Selah*"
> (Psalm 85:2 GW)

Selah. Stop. Pause. Listen.

It isn't hard to miss the message of salvation in this psalm. It is thought that this was written after a remnant of Jews returned to Jerusalem from their seventy-year exile in Babylon. They were exiled because of their sin. They returned with a determination to never worship idols again.

Verses 4-7 are a wonderful prayer asking for forgiveness and restoration. Verses 10-13 show the results of that forgiveness. This message is still for us today. I hope that you take the time to read this salvation psalm.

Salvation isn't just following a set of rules, attending church, hanging out with the right people, wearing the right clothes, or even saying the right words. It isn't about just being a good person either, because Israel did all that.

It's much more. It's about the heart that seeks a relationship with God. "If we say, "We have a relationship with God" and yet live in the dark, we're lying. We aren't being truthful. But if we live in the light in the same way that God is in the light, we have a relationship with each other. And the blood of his Son Jesus cleanses us from every sin. God is faithful and reliable. If we confess our sins, he forgives them and cleanses us from everything we've done wrong." (1 John 1:6-7, 9GW)

The psalmist prayed, "Show us your mercy, O LORD, by giving us your salvation." (Psalm 85:7 GW) That gift of salvation is found only in Jesus, the Son of God. "So, brothers, I'm telling you that through Jesus your sins can be forgiven. Sins kept you from receiving God's approval through Moses' Teachings. However, everyone who believes in Jesus receives God's approval. (Acts 13:38-39 GW)

If you don't have a relationship with God today, start with the simple request to know Him personally, intimately. Admit your guilt, just as the psalmist prayed.

"If you declare that Jesus is Lord, and believe that God brought him back to life, you will be saved. By believing you receive God's approval, and by declaring your faith you are saved." (Romans 10:9-10 GW)

Psalm 87

My heart is so incredibly overwhelmed with joy and excitement as I read this psalm. What a beautiful analogy of the born again Christ follower. It's like coming to the end of the story and seeing how all the pieces fit together. It's the expression of God's redeeming love for us, His Christ followers.

> "On the holy mount stands the city he founded; the LORD loves the gates of Zion more than all the dwelling places of Jacob. Glorious things of you are spoken, O city of God. *Selah*" Psalm 87:1-3 ESV)

Selah. Stop. Pause. Listen.

Zion, another name for Jerusalem, was a fortress on a hill. I find it interesting that Zion is literally translated as "parched place." God chose this barren place for His temple, a place that only He could make beautiful. God had the temple completely covered in gold. It shone like a bright light on the hill for all to see. "You are light for the world. A city cannot be hidden when it is located on a hill." (Matthew 5:14 GW) So, it's never about us; it's always about Him.

Zion wasn't only associated with Jerusalem and the temple, it expanded in meaning over time to include all of Israel. In the New Testament, Zion takes on the spiritual meaning of God's kingdom of all believers from all nations as told in verse 4. "Instead, you have come to Mount Zion, to the city of the living God, to the heavenly Jerusalem. You have come to tens of thousands of angels joyfully gathered together and to the assembly of God's firstborn children (whose names are written in heaven). You have come to a judge (the God of all people) and to the spirits of people who have God's approval and have gained eternal life. You have come to Jesus, who brings the new promise from God, and to the sprinkled blood that speaks a better message than Abel's." (Hebrews 12:22-24 GW)

To get to Zion, you had to go through the gate. Isn't it interesting that the psalmist says that God loves the gates of Zion? The gate was a meeting place for leaders and officials in the Old Testament. Jesus called Himself the Gate. "Jesus emphasized, "I am the gate. Those who enter the sheep pen through me will be saved. They will go in and out of the sheep pen and find food." (John 10:9 GW) There is only one way into God's presence and that is through Jesus. God loves His Gate!

> "The LORD records as he registers the
> peoples, "This one was born there."
> *Selah*" (Psalm 87:6 ESV)

Selah. Stop. Pause. Listen.

As we go through His Gate, Jesus, our name is recorded into the Book of Life like the Shepherd counting his sheep. We become His. Not adopted but born there. He takes our barren, wasted life and turns it lush and full of joy.

As the years have passed and I've lived my life for God, I've lived fully. That's not to say that I haven't had bad times, trials, and hardships, or that I haven't made mistakes along the way. Sometimes I've questioned, not sure where I was headed. I just knew that God asked me to follow. There were times when I doubted and I thought I couldn't go on. There were times when I was scared. But through it all, when I thought that I couldn't hang on any longer, God was there. When life was full of joy and I thought it couldn't get any better, God was there, celebrating with me. I've learned that God is always faithful.

If I've learned nothing else through these years, it is how much God cares. He's laughed with me, cried with me, held on to me, talked with me, and walked with me. I know His incredible, undeniable love for me. I know that my name is in His Book of Life. And I can hardly wait!

I hope that you too have entered through His Gate, Jesus. I hope that you too have His light shining through you and that the world sees it. I hope that you too rejoice and sing and dance because your name is in His Book.

"Singers and dancers alike say, "All my springs are in you." (Psalm 87:7 ESV)

Psalm 88

There was a time in my life when I had lost all trust. I didn't trust family, friends, or God. The pain was so great, so deep, and so all-encompassing that I felt completely alone. I know some of you reading this are thinking "how could she not trust God? Maybe she didn't really know God. If she did, she wouldn't have gone through that time, and certainly would have been more victorious in it. Maybe her faith was weak. Maybe she didn't really believe."

It's not that I didn't believe, because I did, but that I had lost trust. Almost daily during this time I let God know that I didn't trust Him. I could hear Him say, "I know daughter. It's okay. I can wait for however long it takes for you to trust again." Over the next few years, God proved Himself over and over even though He didn't have to. Trust gently returned in its time. "It was good that I had to suffer in order to learn your laws." (Psalm 119:71 GW) I thank God for that broken time of life.

"Your rage lies heavily on me. You make all your waves pound on me. *Selah*. Will you perform miracles for those who are dead? Will the spirits of the dead rise and give thanks to you? *Selah*" (Psalm 88:7, 10 GW)

Selah. Stop. Pause. Listen.

This psalm is probably one of the saddest of the whole book. It is a deep, pain filled, gut wrenching cry of the heart. There is no joy, no hope of any kind, no looking for saving. He expresses a depth of pain and confusion so great that he despairs of life and asks God why. It doesn't end with any great revelation of who God is or His care or anything redeeming about his circumstances. I can sympathize with the pain and emptiness that he felt as he penned these words.

What we do read is that he knew God was listening. He didn't sugar coat his feelings with pious words. He told God exactly how he felt.

So, go ahead and tell God. Are you angry at God? Tell Him. Confused? Tell Him. Do you feel abandoned, alone, hard done by? It's okay. Tell Him. He is listening. My God is big enough to handle your truest feelings.

Getting this real with God takes courage. Sometimes it isn't about trust or faith, but about real courage. God can handle the ugly truth of your pain. And when you are real, God can walk with you through the pain, the doubt, the loss, and bring you through to the other side. And when you are on the other side of your deep pain, you will look back and see the way He carried you through. You will have a deeper, stronger, and closer relationship with God. Suffering is inevitable in this life. So is God.

> "God, who shows you his kindness and who has called you through Christ Jesus to his eternal glory, will restore you, strengthen you, make you strong, and support you as you suffer for a little while. Power belongs to him forever. Amen." (1 Peter 5:10-11 GW)

Psalm 89

My life has often felt like a yo-yo. I seem to go from the highest of highs to deepest of lows, often with not much transition time in between. One day I'm praising God for all He is, all He has done, and how wonderful being with Him is. Then, something goes awry, and I'm plunged into doubt, confusion, and despair wondering how this happened, did I do something wrong, and why me. I just don't do life easily, but I wouldn't change a thing. I think I'm mellowing, but I would have to ask Brian about that. He'll just smile, knowing better than to answer such a loaded question from his wife.

I can relate with the writer of this Psalm with its high and low. It is prophetic looking toward Christ and relevant for our life today. Let's look at the three Selahs of this psalm.

> "I will sing forever about the evidence
> of your mercy, O LORD. I will tell about
> your faithfulness to every generation.

I said, "Your mercy will last forever. Your faithfulness stands firm in the heavens." You said, "I have made a promise to my chosen one. I swore this oath to my servant David: 'I will make your dynasty continue forever. I built your throne to last throughout every generation.' " *Selah*" (Psalm 89:1-4)

Selah. Stop. Pause. Listen.

It isn't hard to see the incredible joy that the psalmist has in these opening verses. He sings of God's faithfulness and the promise to him and future generations of a lasting kingdom. For the next twenty-five verses he continues his song of praise. When life is good it's really, really good.

The next sixteen verses aren't so joyous though. "You cut short the days of his youth and covered him with shame. *Selah*" (Psalm 89:45 GW)

Selah. Stop. Pause. Listen.

Speaking prophetically of the sufferings of Christ these also tell of a broken relationship with God and its results. The pointing fingers, the whispers behind the back, this is a person that is remembered not for their accomplishments but for their failures. We don't want to think that God would actually allow us to go through hardship. That just doesn't sound very loving.

If Jesus hadn't gone through the cross, we wouldn't have a means of a relationship with God. If we don't go through sufferings, we may not develop a real and close relationship with God. God loves us enough to allow us to fall down, get hurt, cry, and then pick us up when the time is ready. That is how we grow and learn. "Let's return to the LORD. Even though he has torn us to pieces, he will heal us. Even though he has wounded us, he will bandage our wounds." (Hosea 6:1 GW)

In his pain and confusion and seeking answers, the psalmist asks "Can a mortal go on living and never see death? Who can set himself free from the power of the grave? *Selah*" (Psalm 89:48-49 GW)

Selah. Stop. Pause. Listen.

The answer is found in Jesus Christ. Only Jesus has risen from the dead and lives today. Today, we know the answer to the questions. That was the psalmist's hope then and is yours today.

The final verses of this psalm are worth closing with. "Remember, O LORD, how your servant has been insulted. Remember how I have carried in my heart the insults from so many people. Your enemies insulted me. They insulted your Messiah every step he took. Thank the LORD forever. Amen and amen!" (Psalm 89:50-52 GW)

Jesus felt all the pain and rejection, so will you. He knows how you feel. Praise God when you are going through wonderful happy times. Enjoy them and thank God for them. But know that difficult times are also a part of your walk with God.

> "My brothers and sisters, be very happy when you are tested in different ways. You know that such testing of your faith produces endurance. Endure until your testing is over. Then you will be mature and complete, and you won't need anything." (James 1:2-4 GW)

Psalm 140

I like David. He had such a real relationship with God. He was always ready to "tell it like it is" to God. Many of my conversations with God sound a lot like his. I like to get right to the point when I talk with God. I have never been one to try and convince God about what He should do or think of a situation. I know that He already is well aware of my problem. I never learned to flatter, instead I learned to worship. So, I talk. Then I listen. Then I am comforted. I know He has heard my cry. I know that He is in control. So whether or not I have to walk through the trial, I know that God is with me, guiding, protecting, and teaching.

Being king, David had many enemies, often within his own house. As I read this psalm I couldn't help but see parallels to much of what we as Christ followers are beginning to feel. There are many countries where the mention of the name of God is dangerous to a believer. We have been spared much of that in the Western World. But the day is coming.

We can glean a lot from this psalm penned by David about those who would try to entrap and discredit us.

> "Rescue me from evil people, O LORD. Keep me safe from violent people. They plan evil things in their hearts. They start fights every day. They make their tongues as sharp as a snake's fang. Their lips hide the venom of poisonous snakes. Selah. Arrogant people have laid a trap for me. They have spread out a net with ropes. They have set traps for me along the road. *Selah*" (1-3, 5 GW)

Selah. Stop. Pause. Listen.

Have you ever felt like what you say gets twisted? No matter how you say it, the wrong meaning is attached to it. You want to stand for righteousness, truth, and justice. Instead, you are deemed narrow minded, unloving, and prejudiced.

So what do you do? David's first line of defense was to turn to God. David didn't start his prayer with praise, thanks, or any flowery words. He got right to the point. He prayed rescue me and keep me safe. Then he told God, in his own words, what was going on.

There are times when only the urgent prayer is possible. You don't have time to run to your prayer closet or prayer group. You need help now. You need peace and direction right now. Go ahead. Tell it like it is. God is listening. He cares and He knows.

"I said to the LORD, "You are my God." O LORD, open your ears to hear my plea for pity. O LORD Almighty, the strong one who saves me, you have covered my head in the day of battle. O LORD, do not give wicked people what they want. Do not let their evil plans succeed, or they will become arrogant. *Selah*" (Psalm 140:6-8 GW)

Selah. Stop. Pause. Listen.

I like the shift of his prayer in these verses. David speaks words of affirmation, to God as much as to himself. David reminds himself of his relationship with God and God's protection over him. He calls Him my God, Lord Almighty, the strong one who saves me, and you cover my head in battle.

As you pray, remember who God is for you. He is Provider, Rescuer, Lover, Protector, All Powerful, The One Who Sees, and the names go on. Let Him know what He means to you. Remember God; remember why you trusted Him with your life. Remember how He has helped you, comforted you, restored you, and watched over you.

Times are coming when your faith and trust in God will be challenged. Will you choose to stand firm with the saints who have gone before you against the lies that are hurled at you? Will you allow God to defend you? You may not get the outcome you desire here and now, but you will get the reward in eternity. "I know that the LORD will defend the rights of those who are oppressed and the cause of those who are needy. Indeed, righteous people will give thanks to your name. Decent people will live in your presence." (Psalm 140:12-13 GW)

> "Don't look to men for help; their greatest leaders fail; for every man must die. His breathing stops, life ends, and in a moment all he planned for himself is ended. But happy is the man who has the God of Jacob as his helper, whose hope is in the Lord his God—the God who made both earth and heaven, the seas and everything in them. He is the God who keeps every promise," (Psalm 146:3-6 TLB)

Psalm 143

Have you ever been asked the question if you had the chance to do it over again, what would you do differently? It's the great "what if" question that most of us have thought about at one time or another, especially when life is overwhelming.

There are many fiction movies and books about just such a possibility. As the hero goes back in time to correct one supposed mistake, another takes its place. The outcome is almost always worse than if no change had been made. It becomes painfully obvious that he can't change the past.

Now, the older, somewhat wiser me knows there is nothing that I would change. I wouldn't be me if I did. I love who I've become. I praise God for who I am in Him. I've journeyed through sorrow, loss, and pain. I've rejoiced with joy, hope, and peace. I remember the times of intimate uninterrupted worship and prayer. I see the times when God held on to me because I couldn't hang on to Him. I remember the quiet place of restoration where soul and body were made whole again. What a wonderful place of rest and restoration it was. But life called and I was now prepared to face it again. I see the child I was and the woman of God I have become. I have journeyed with God, and it isn't over yet. I know there is so much more to come!

> "I remember the days long ago. I reflect on all that you have done. I carefully consider what your hands have made. I stretch out my hands to you in prayer. Like parched land, my soul thirsts for you. *Selah*" (Psalm 143:5-6 GW)

Selah. Stop. Pause. Listen.

The last Selah. Isn't it interesting? I find it appropriate to end this journey with these two verses. What are we encouraged to do? Remember. Reflect. Carefully consider. Raise your hands in prayer. Thirst for God.

Sometimes part of the Selah is to stop and pause and look back on your journey. Sometimes, like David, you need to look back to see how far you have come. Take a good look. Reflect.

I would like to leave you with a few questions to help you reflect on your journey.

How has your relationship with God grown? Do you see how God has led you, fed you, protected you, and taught you? Do you understand why He allowed you to make your mistakes and the growth that happened because of them?

Has God become an intricate part of your life? Is God the litmus test for all you do, where you go, and what you say and believe? Are you separate from the world, or do you still try to live with one foot in the world and one with God?

As you look back, look forward. There is so much more journey ahead of you. As David did, raise your hands in prayer and praise. Be thirsty for the only One who can satisfy you.

Let us say with Paul, "I no longer live, but Christ lives in me. The life I now live I live by believing in God's Son, who loved me and took the punishment for my sins." (Galatians 2:20 GW)

Selah. Stop Pause. Listen.

Remember in your life to Stop now and again. Hit the Pause button long enough to focus on God. Then Listen for His still small voice as he speaks to your heart.

"This is the person who seeks him, who searches for the face of the God of Jacob. *Selah*" (Psalm 24:6 GW)

About the Author

Wendy Miller Bartsch was born and raised in New Jersey. She spent her early adult years in Northern BC Canada serving in missions and raising her children. Numerous moves and life challenges deepened her faith and trust in God. With a heart after God, she serves wherever God plants her. Always looking for a creative challenge, she started writing devotionals and posting them to Facebook. With much encouragement from family and friends this book was created. She now resides in Fort St John, BC with her husband. Together they have six children, ten grandchildren, and one great-grandchild.

CPSIA information can be obtained
at www.ICGtesting.com
Printed in the USA
BVHW090826071022
648775BV00006B/17

9 781662 856044